SWIMMING AND WATER SAFETY
TEXTBOOK

With 220 illustrations

First Edition

1968

The American National Red Cross
Washington, D.C. 20006

THE MISSION OF THE RED CROSS

The American Red Cross is the instrument chosen by the Congress to help carry out the obligations assumed by the United States under certain international treaties known as the Geneva or Red Cross Conventions. Specifically, its congressional charter imposes on the American Red Cross the duties to act as the medium of voluntary relief and communication between the American people and their armed forces, and to carry on a system of national and international relief to prevent and mitigate suffering caused by disasters.

All the activities of the American Red Cross and its chapters support these duties.

Nationally and locally the American Red Cross is governed by volunteers, most of its duties are performed by volunteers and it is financed by voluntary contributions.

The Lifesaving and Water Safety programs of the American National Red Cross, for which this book is a teaching text, stem from the congressional charter provision that the organization shall devise and carry on measures for relieving and preventing suffering.

Third Printing March 1971

Copyright © 1968 by
The American National Red Cross
All Rights Reserved
Library of Congress Catalog Card No. 68-25833

All illustrations reproduced in Chapter 8, "Diving," are reprinted from Anne Ross Fairbanks' Teaching Springboard Diving, *© 1963, by permission of the author and Prentice-Hall, Inc., Englewood Cliffs, New Jersey.*

Printed in the United States of America

PREFACE

Swimming and water safety instruction continues to be the most fundamental part of the American Red Cross total water safety program. Anyone who swims reasonably well and in addition possesses a sufficient number of safety skills should be able to take care of himself in most water emergencies. Without skilled swimmers, there could be no lifesaving training program because one should be a capable swimmer before he can acquire the skills necessary for making a swimming rescue. Furthermore, the ability to swim must be a prerequisite for active participation in such aquatic activities as sailing, boating, canoeing, water skiing, surfing, and skin and scuba diving.

When Commodore Wilbert E. Longfellow started the Life Saving Service of the American Red Cross in 1914, he recognized the need for providing swimming instruction as a part of the water safety program. In an attempt to meet this need, nonswimmers were taught simple skills in a mass instruction approach. By 1934, it had become evident that too many beginners did not have an opportunity of progressing beyond this level and, in fact, had probably learned to swim just enough to get into trouble.

In 1938, the American Red Cross published the textbook *Swimming and Diving* as the resource that would enable water safety instructors to teach a program of swimming courses that started at the beginner level and progressed through the advanced swimmer level. For 25 years, this text was used as the technical reference for all Red Cross swimming instruction in this country and it filled a great need.

The level, scope, and knowledge of aquatics have risen rapidly since 1938, and, in an attempt to keep pace with the increased interest and activity, the American Red Cross has published this new textbook. The task of "waterproofing" America is still a major challenge. Each year, well over 100 million Americans actively engage in some form of aquatic recreation and many millions still cannot swim or swim so poorly that they are frequently in danger of drowning. In fact, *everyone* should know how to swim because yearly drowning statistics prove that over 60 percent of drowning fatalities occur to people who accidentally find themselves in the water.

This book, developed by Edmond J. Mongeon, national director of the American Red Cross Water Safety Program, is dedicated to the great task of teaching and learning the art of swimming and water safety. It is the textbook for Red Cross swimming instructional courses. At the same time, it is an authoritative resource for all swimming instructors and provides information useful to all persons interested in furthering safety in, on, or around the water.

ACKNOWLEDGMENTS

The American Red Cross wishes to acknowledge with appreciation the contributions made by Carroll L. Bryant and Richard L. Brown, former directors of its Water Safety Program. Much of the material is based on the 1938 textbook *Swimming and Diving*, which was written by Mr. Bryant, and on the information contained in a variety of instructor guides and manuals later written by Mr. Brown.

Special acknowledgement and thanks are extended to the following review committee: Mrs. Prudence Fleming, Associate Professor, Health and Physical Education, Temple University; Mrs. Mary Kinman, Assistant Professor, Health and Physical Education, William Jewell College; Louis A. Parker, Head Swimming Coach, George Washington High School, Denver, Colorado; Jack Ryan, Coach of Swimming, U.S. Military Academy; Walter J. Schlueter, Head Swimming Coach, Arizona State University.

In addition to their school affiliations, the above committee represented the following aquatic organizations: Division for Girls and Women's Sports of the American Association of Health, Physical Education and Recreation; Women's National Aquatic Forum; National Interscholastic Swimming Coaches Association; College Swimming Coaches Association; and American Swimming Coaches Association.

The findings and recommendations of this review group, which, in conference, examined the manuscript thoroughly, contributed greatly to this publication.

An advisory committee of the College Swimming Coaches Association comprised of Joseph R. Rogers, Jr., Mark Randall, and Irving Simone met in conference with the writer during the initial planning stage of the textbook, and its suggestions concerning format, content, resources, and procedures to follow were very helpful.

Special thanks is extended to Prof. Charles E. Silvia of Springfield College, Massachusetts, for contributing the basic information that is contained in Chapter 4, "Physical Laws Governing Body Movements in the Water."

Gratitude is expressed to those American Red Cross Water Safety professional staff members who also met as a review committee, studied the manuscript, and gave valuable advice and recommendations. The writer has drawn heavily upon the experience of many Red Cross professional and volunteer water safety staff in the field and at national headquarters and of other aquatic specialists as well. The advice and the cooperation of all these individuals are greatly appreciated.

CONTENTS

Chapter 1. The Evolution of Swimming 1

Chapter 2. Teaching the Beginning Swimmer—Using Artificial Supports. Learning Sequences. 9

Chapter 3. Guidelines for Teaching Different Age Levels—Working With Preschool Children. Working With Elementary School-Age Children. Working With Teen-agers. Working With Adults. 36

Chapter 4. Physical Laws Governing Body Movements in the Water—Bouyancy. Motion. Leverage. Relaxation. Breathing. Other Factors To Be Considered. 43

Chapter 5. Analysis of Basic Swimming Strokes—Sidestroke. Elementary Backstroke. Breaststroke. Crawl Stroke. Back Crawl. 52

Chapter 6. Additional Strokes and Variations—Overarm Sidestroke. Trudgen Strokes. Inverted Breaststroke. Butterfly Stroke. 70

Chapter 7. Related Aquatic Skills—Surface Diving. Sculling. Treading Water. Underwater Swimming. Front Start (Shallow Dive). Starting on the Back. Turns. 78

Chapter 8. Diving—Diving Fundamentals. Diving Safety. Progression for the Beginner. Standing Front Dive From Board. Running Front Dive From Board. 97

Chapter 9. Safety in Aquatics—Personal Water Safety. Safety at Home Pools. Safety at Farm Ponds. Safety at Beaches. Helping Others in an Emergency. Helping Yourself in an Emergency. Survival Floating. 110

Chapter 10. Fun in Fundamentals—Selection of Activity. Individual Contests and Stunts at the Beginner and Advanced Beginner Levels. Group Games and Contests at the Beginner Level. Team Games for All Levels. Mass Games. Relay Races. 128

Chapter 11. Artificial Respiration—Artificial Respiration for Water Cases. Related Information. 138

1

THE EVOLUTION OF SWIMMING

As practiced by man, swimming is an art. Fish, amphibia, waterfowl, and practically all quadrupeds are either born with the ability to swim, have instincts that enable them to acquire swimming ability very rapidly, or are able to use the same form of locomotion in water as they do on land and still make good progress.

Basically, man is handicapped by structure and habit when he enters the water. His natural position is upright and he propels himself by thrusting against the ground with a relatively small area of the foot. Also, for the most part, he possesses a narrow margin of buoyancy. The specific gravity of a human being is so nearly that of water itself that the average man, when suspended motionless in the water, finds that he submerges to about eye level. Unable to breathe at this level, he must necessarily make some lifting motions to raise himself a little above his normal flotation level. If, in this vertical position, he attempts to make progress by using the same movements as walking on land, it can only result in possibly some up and down movement but little or no forward progress. Man must therefore adjust to water as an element, learn to assume other than the vertical position, and finally employ different arm and leg movements.

In spite of not being an amphibious animal, man has become amazingly versatile in the water primarily because of his capacity to reason plus having an important physical asset. This asset is a set of swivel or ball and socket joints in shoulders and hips that permit a wide range of movement. As a result, he can swim on the front, on the side, and on the back, at the surface or underneath. He can swim forward, backward, or even sidewise. He can somersault forward or backward or can rotate on the long axis of the body like a rolling log. In contrast, swimming animals are limited by their structure to far fewer patterns of swimming action.

Even though man has devised a great variety of skills and stunts and has given them names such as dolphin, porpoise, seal-diving, swordfish, sealfish, marlin, and many others, the physical action employed by man is radically different from that of the animals that gave the skills their names. There is actually little that man has been able to borrow from the animal world in the development of the art of swimming. However, until this fact was understood, it acted as a deterrent in the development of man's progress in the water. A classic example is the kick employed in the breaststroke. All through history, learners were told to imitate the frog in using the legs for this stroke. However, when man attempts to thrust backward against the water as the frog does with his widespreading, webbed feet, he gets little forward progress. Yet even today the leg action in the breaststroke is mistakenly called the frog kick.

Through a slow process over the centuries, man has had to learn and discover his own principles and methods of water locomotion. Man has learned from his predecessors, but for many years improvement was the result of trial and error only. During the modern era, improved facilities, clarity of water, photographic techniques permitting stop action and slow motion filming of body movements in the water, especially under the surface, have all enhanced the understanding of how man swims most effectively. Scientific study and experimentation by qualified swimming experts have resulted in applying the physical laws that govern body movements in the water to the point where man today is swimming more efficiently and effectively than ever before.

How and why man actually took to the water is not known. However, the three motivating forces that influenced his immersion were undoubtedly economic necessity, comfort, and preservation of life in the face of danger. Economic necessity must have been the dominant factor. Man derived much of his food supply from the many forms of marine life. Wading, reaching, and groping for food in shallow waters caused initial immersion and paved the way for the development of some forms of swimming movement. Seeking to escape the discomfort caused by extreme heat, during hot seasons and in tropical regions, man must have discovered early in his experience that immersion in water allayed that discomfort. Immersion could also have been used by primitive man as a refuge from fire, animals, and fellowmen in an attempt to preserve his own life when in danger. Other motivations may have been cleanliness, immersion as a religious rite, and possibly for sport.

Prior to 1500 A.D., there is only fragmentary evidence on the art of swimming. Ancient literature contains many references to swimming indicating that it was well known to the ancients and commonly used among people of many races. Tales of great feats of swimming prowess are recorded in the sagas of Scandinavia, in the English epic poem *Beowulf,* and in certain Greek and Roman classics, but in every case it is the feat itself and not the swimming technique that is described. In the Nimrud Gallery of the British Museum are a series of excellent bas-reliefs that were discovered in the Nimrud Palace in Assyria by the English archeologist Sir Austin Henry Layard. These bas-reliefs, all depicting swimming figures, are assigned to about 880 B.C. Most of these are of military motive, depicting scenes of battle in which soldiers are shown crossing streams. In many cases, they are shown swimming with the aid of a mussuk, an inflated goat or sheep skin. With the mussuk clasped against the chest with one arm, the figures are using a vertical kick and a hand-over-hand stroke with the free arm. A number of these are depicted without the support of a mussuk, swimming an unmistakable hand-over-hand stroke. It is reasonable to suppose that, because of military necessity, the highly civilized Assyrians developed a fair degree of swimming proficiency and when possible used the mussuk as a buoyant aid primarily because of the weight of their fighting garments and equipment.

This style of swimming probably extended to the people inhabiting the lands of the Eastern Mediterranean through the many invasions of Assyria. There is evidence that the Greeks and, later, the Romans, used a hand-over-hand stroke. To cite two examples, there is preserved in the British Museum the "Coin of Abydos," depicting Leander swimming a hand-over-hand style across the Hellespont while Hero, standing in her tower with a lighted lamp, indicates the way. This coin of the ancient Greeks is dated A.D. 193. On still another fragment, a painting found on a wall of a ruined house in Pompeii, there is a depiction of Leander swimming the hand-over-hand stroke, proving definitely that the stroke was known to the ancient Romans.

While there is fragmentary evidence in literature and the visual arts that ancient peoples swam, prior to the sixteenth century no one, presumably, thought it necessary to describe the strokes used or any method of teaching. At that point, however, a few treatises on swimming began to appear in the literature of Europe. The first known work on swimming was written by Nicolaus Wynman, a German professor of languages, and was published in 1538. In 1587, a book on swimming, written in Latin by Sir Everard Digby and later translated into English, was published in England. About 1697, a Frenchman, Thevenot, wrote a book entitled *The Art of Swimming*, in which he described and illustrated a method closely resembling the breaststroke. This style of swimming gave unobstructed vision and, with the mouth and nose held out of water, permitted free breathing. The underwater arm recovery eliminated splashing water in the swimmer's face and gave the swimmer good stability even in rough water. From Thevenot's description it is evident that a breaststroke style had been in common usage for many years. English translations of his work became a standard reference and helped to establish this stroke as the method most commonly employed, a distinction it was to enjoy for many years.

From this point, the people of northern Europe went through a process of evolving a series of swimming strokes, turning from the breast to the side and progressing to an overarm sidestroke used extensively in England in the middle nineteenth century. With the introduction of competition, speed became an important factor and the hand-over-hand stroke came, belatedly, to Europe. It was introduced in England, in 1873, by John Trudgen, who had learned the style from South American Indians. This hand-over-hand stroke, also referred to as the alternating overarm stroke, soon caught the public fancy and was actually the forerunner in the development of the crawl stroke as it is known today. Each arm recovered out of water by rolling the body from side to side and evidently a scissors kick occurred following the stroke of each arm.

Until approximately the turn of the 20th century, most of the attention had been given to arm action, with almost total disregard of the action of the legs. Now, however, the increasing emphasis on competition spurred a search for styles of swimming and refinements in stroking that would produce even greater speed over measured distances than the trudgen stroke. Study and experimentation with the trudgen showed that negative recovery action of the legs discounted much of the positive thrust. Each leg kick provided a single forward thrust, and, finally, the kick did not seem to blend with the alternating overarm stroke.

At this point, an Australian competitive swimmer, Richard Cavill, developed an up and down thrashing action of the legs that he combined with the alternating overarm stroke. This style was introduced in 1902 at the International Championships, where Cavill demonstrated its speed by swimming 100 yards in 58.4 seconds to set a new world record. The method became known as the Australian Crawl, and with this introduction of a form of the flutter kick a new era in speed swimming began.

American swimming coaches and speed swimmers made

further refinements in the breathing, kicking, and arm recovery techniques of the crawl. The success of their efforts was evident when, in 1906, C. M. Daniels became the first United States speed swimming champion of the world as he lowered the 100-yard record to 55.4. The Australian Crawl, with refinements, became known as the American Crawl.

The development of the crawl stroke was further influenced by the late "Duke" Kahanamoku, a Hawaiian, whose stroke was featured by a truly vertical, 6-beat flutter kick action of the legs. The "Duke" was an Olympic record holder and Olympic Gold Medal winner for 100 yards in both the 1912 and 1920 Games. Also influencing the stroke was another outstanding U.S. swimmer, Johnny Weissmuller, who dominated crawl sprint swimming throughout the years encompassing the 1924 and 1928 Olympic Games. In 1927, Weissmuller swam 100 yards in 51 seconds flat in a 25-yard course, setting a record that was to remain unbroken for almost two decades. Weissmuller's style featured a deeper kick that allowed the chest and shoulders to ride higher, a rotating of the head, for inhalation, that was independent of the action of the arms, and an underwater arm action in which the elbow was bent slightly for greater positive action. Since champions have always had a large following, the popularity of both Duke Kahanamoku and Johnny Weissmuller not only contributed greatly to the development of the present-day crawl but popularized the stroke so that it became the stroke to teach beginners.

During the 1920's the Japanese made extensive use of slow-motion films that were taken of Weissmuller and other great swimmers to add further improvements to stroking mechanics. These improvements, coupled with a tremendous emphasis on training and conditioning, enabled the Japanese to dominate swimming in the early thirties.

In the present day, more people are swimming for pleasure and more people are competing than ever before, and the continuing lowering of swimming records is indicative that stroking mechanics are still being improved.

Prior to about 1900, swimming on the back was more a stunt then an actual stroke. Since the breaststroke was in high favor at the turn of the century, the stroke on the back that was performed at that time was a breaststroke inverted. With the development of the alternating overarm style on the front, this method was experimented with on the back and finally, combined with an inverted flutter kick, resulted in a stroke that was faster than the breaststroke. In 1912, the backstroke was recognized as a competitive event. The search for greater speed, combined with basically the same elements of study and experimentation that occurred in the development of the crawl stroke, has led to the refinements of the stroke as we know it today.

The history of the breaststroke is interesting and again points to the influence of speed swimming in its development. Even though other strokes were proved to be faster, the breaststroke has continued as a separate competitive event. In fact, until the recognition of the butterfly stroke as a separate stroke in competition, the breaststroke was the only one in which a prescribed style was required. However, since the breaststroke employed an underwater recovery of both arms and legs, this high resistance factor was a problem in developing more speed. In 1934, David Armbruster, then swimming coach at the University of Iowa, devised a variation that employed a double overarm recovery out of water. This arm action resulted in greater speed but required greater training and conditioning. In 1935, a breaststroke style was introduced that incorporated the out-of-water arm recovery combined with a vertical dolphin or fishtail kick. Even though this was a faster method of the butterfly, this dolphin kick was declared in violation of the competitive rules.

For the next 20 years, champion breaststrokers used an out-of-water arm recovery (butterfly) with a shortened breaststroke kick. In the late 1950's, the butterfly with the dolphin kick was legalized for competition, and the butterfly stroke and the breaststroke were then separated into two distinctly different strokes.

It can be seen that the quest for speed has greatly influenced how man swims. By applying the same basic body mechanics that the competitive swimmer uses and by taking advantage of the experience and knowledge gained over the years, the noncompetitor should become a safer and more effective performer in the water.

2

TEACHING THE BEGINNING SWIMMER

Learning how to swim should be kept enjoyable regardless of the age of the learner. It must be a gradual process. Proper motivation is important, and, above all, the safety of the learner should be paramount.

Some specific information will be geared to the problems encountered in teaching various age levels, but, for all groups, the major obstacle or problem that must be overcome is the physical and mental adjustment to submerging the face and body in water. This initial adjustment involves the important step of submerging with the face underwater and holding the breath without discomfort.

In order to perfect the adjustment skills, the learner will usually require a great deal of practice time. When complete adjustment and breath control have not been mastered, the beginner may learn to propel himself and make some progress with his head out of water but the individual will never be safe. Also, the beginner's progress will be hindered because of poor body position and balance that will result from the high head position. Generally, the more time spent in becoming thoroughly adjusted to the water, the faster and safer will be the progress toward becoming a skilled performer.

While there are certain fundamental skills that should be taught at the beginning swimmer level, there is flexibility concerning the order of their presentation. Also, it should not be construed that an instructor teaches one battery of skills and then graduates to the next series in a specific transition. One instructor may teach a prone float, a skill in the buoyancy and body position series, and then immediately introduce the prone glide, one of the skills of propulsion. Another may wish to teach the various floating positions before adding the glide. There may be an integration of skills from the various sequences as well as a repeating process of practicing many skills listed in an earlier sequence. Personal safety and simple assists, for example, should be woven into the total beginner instruction.

All instructors must realize the necessity of using a different approach with various age groups (see chapter 3) and of adapting the teaching progressions to the facility as well as to the capabilities of aides when such personnel are available. When instruction is given in constant-depth pools of 3-3½ feet, the skills of entry, such as jumping into deep water and diving, may have to be necessarily postponed until a facility with deeper water can be used. However, the initial steps of a jump entry and of diving from a sitting position can usually be practiced by children.

Using Artificial Supports

In addition to stationary supports such as the side of the pool or a kicking rail, there are three broad categories of artificial supports used in teaching beginners.

HAND SUPPORT

The hand support by the instructor or an aide is very important during the adjustment phase and is especially helpful in working with young children. This personal contact helps give the learner confidence and, with the possible exception of free-floating supports, is the only support used by many instructors.

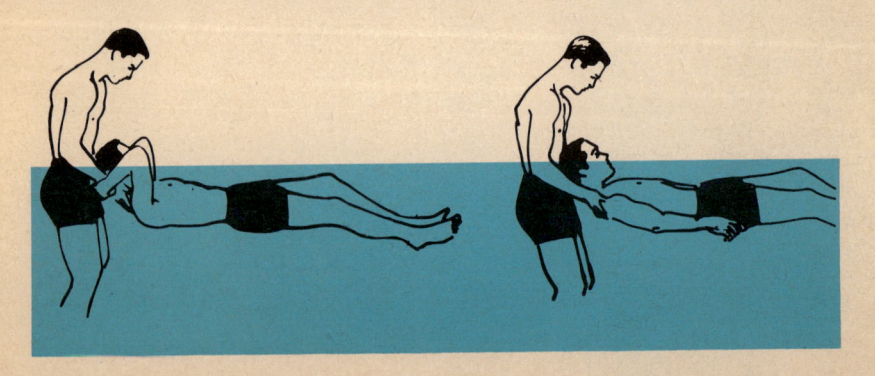

FREE-FLOATING SUPPORT

The free-floating support gives the user some added buoyancy but is not attached to the body and can be moved from place to place. Swimboards, or kickboards, and cannisters are examples of this type of support. Such supports are generally accepted for assisting the learner when he is practicing parts of a stroke, such as kicking, using the arms only, and coordinated stroking.

SUPPORT ATTACHED TO THE BODY

Water wings, cannister-type floats, and life preservers are examples of the support attached to the body. It is recommended that, if such supports are used, their use be postponed until the beginner has made a satisfactory mental and physical adjustment to the water. When used after this adjustment, this type of support can be helpful in getting the beginner to maintain a good practicing or working position in the water and, in addition, can enable him to continue a series of practicing movements longer in order to develop patterns of movement. Judicious use of such supports can speed up the learning and make practice sessions more rewarding and meaningful.

Learning Sequences

The sequences involved at the beginning swimming level are physical and mental adjustment, buoyancy and body position, propulsion and coordinated stroking, entries, personal safety, and elementary forms of rescue.

PHYSICAL AND MENTAL ADJUSTMENT

When a nonswimmer enters the water for the first time, he goes through a new and unique experience that requires considerable adjustment to be made both physically and mentally. The water is cool, much colder than the bath water he is accustomed to. Even water temperature of 80°-82°F. will feel cool on the body and cause the breath and pulse to quicken. When the body is submerged in neck-deep water by either wading or crouching, the learner will experience some slight difficulty in breathing because of water pressure and, secondly, he will feel a noticeable loss of weight due to body buoyancy. The effects of temperature, pressure, and buoyancy are the first experiences that the nonswimmer must adjust to.

Many nonswimmers will have some fear of the new element. Most fears are unfounded but are real to the individual. The first step in the adjustment process should be to dissipate this fear and instill confidence. The nonswimmer should understand that he will be in the shallow water area until he is able to swim and that his safety will be protected at all times. If the learner is old enough to understand, it should be clearly explained and demonstrated that he possesses a certain amount of body buoyancy that will help him to stay on the top of the water. Emphasis should also be placed on the ease and simplicity of swimming. In addition, the learner must be impressed with the fact that he will learn if he will follow the instructor's directions and will try the skills and new experiences without hesitation. When the instructor has succeeded in getting the beginner to overcome his fear of the water and to have confidence in him, he has made a good beginning that can do much toward shortening the learning process.

Entering the Water

If there is a gradual slope, ramp, or steps, the learner can wade to about thigh-deep water, scoop water with his hands, and then wet down his arms, chest, neck, and face, thus gradually getting wet all over.

At poolside, the same process of getting wet all over gradually can be accomplished by having the class sit on the edge of the pool deck, reach over, and go through the wetting down process. The class should then be shown how to lower themselves into the water, which in many cases will be neck or chin deep. In such cases, some assistance from the instructor or an aide may be advisable.

There are many adjustment activities that can be done if the water is shallow enough. For example: Sitting on the bottom and with his hands placed behind him, the learner may tilt slightly backward and let the legs rise. Still in the same depth water, he may attempt to lean back and submerge the head as far as the ears. He may roll from the back position to the side and then to the front position and even splash and kick with his legs. He may crawl along the bottom and then add a kicking movement. All of these simple skills should be repeated a number of times since they help the nonswimmer get the "feel" of the water and can give him a feeling of initial accomplishment.

In pools, another skill for the nonswimmer is simply walking in water that may be chest or neck deep. This may have to be initiated by having the pupil keep one hand on the pool side or overflow.

Next, he should try to walk without holding on to the side of the pool. In some cases, instructor help and guidance may be advisable. The walking phase should progress to the point where it is done with both arms and hands in the water to assist in maintaining better balance. Simple walking races are recommended.

Adjustment activities are helpful two ways. They make the water fun for the nonswimmer. In addition, they unconsciously involve him in a series of simple skills in the performance of which he is learning a great deal about adjustment, buoyancy, and body balance.

Breath Holding

With the face out of water, breathing is an instinctive and normal process. To breathe regularly while the face is in the water has to be taught and practiced many times before it becomes instinctive. It should be taught in easy stages with a great deal of practice at every lesson. The process involves breath holding with the face submerged, exhaling underwater, bobbing, opening the eyes underwater, and, finally, rhythmic breathing, a combination of all these skills.

Breath holding that will lead into rhythmic breathing should be introduced early in the learner's experience and should continue to be a regular part of every practice session. The initial objective is to get the nonswimmer to submerge the face and head and to hold his breath comfortably while underwater.

The first step is simply to take a normal breath, close the mouth, and slowly lower the head parallel to the water until at least the face and ears are submerged. When children are hesitant to take this step, the instructor can have them cup water in their hands and then wash and rinse their faces.

Familiarity with the process in using a home washbasin may help children overcome their initial reluctance. The submerging-of-the-face-and-head skill should be repeated many times, and as soon as possible the number of seconds that the head stays submerged should be gradually increased.

The next step is learning how to exhale in the water. Learners can practice by inhaling, compressing the lips, and forcibly exhaling in a manner similar to blowing out a candle. This method of exhalation tends to give better control, stresses breathing out through the mouth, and keeps water from entering the mouth. While some air may be exhaled through the nose, emphasis should be on exhaling through the mouth.

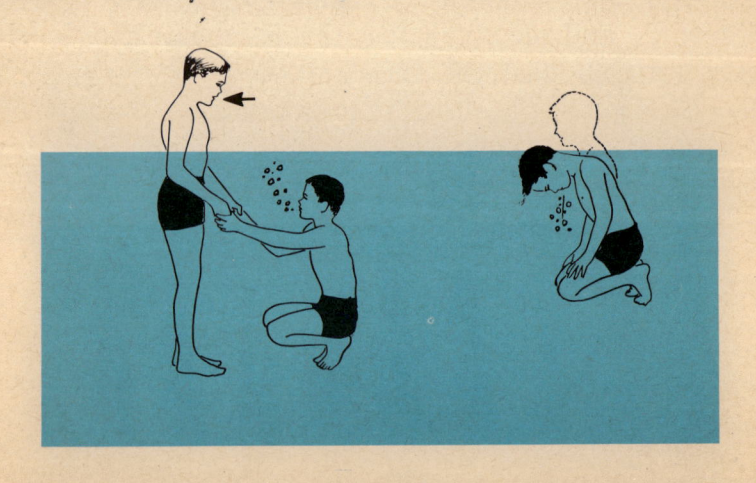

Games and walking races where the learners blow a Ping-Pong ball or balloon in front of their mouths can help at this stage. The use of such graphic descriptions as "blowing bubbles" and "blowing out the candle" will prove helpful here. Learners can be paired off during practice to give added confidence, and after a few attempts the process can be repeated until the rhythmical inhalation and exhalation becomes easier and can be repeated many times.

Seeing Underwater

Interspersed with breath control skills is practice in opening the eyes underwater. The beginner has a tendency to keep the eyes tightly closed, but experience will quickly prove that one is able to see quite well underwater and even enjoy it. Vision will be somewhat blurred; however, exercises such as counting the extended fingers of a partner and locating and retrieving objects in shallow water will help the learner to adjust. For convenience, balance, orientation, and safety, keeping the eyes open when the face is underwater is a must.

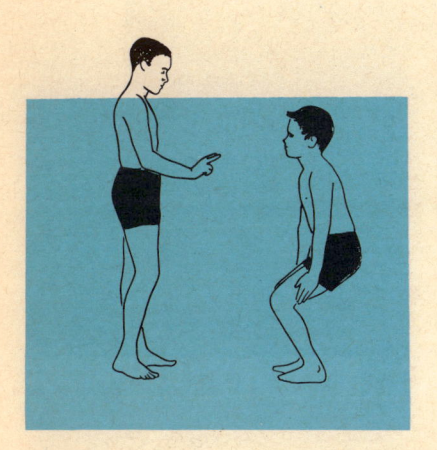

Rhythmic Breathing

Rhythmic breathing is simply breathing in series or in a specific rhythm—inhaling through the mouth as the face is turned to the side and exhaling underwater after the face is turned downward. Adequate ventilation of the lungs at regular intervals is vital to continuous swimming, and breathing practice should be started early in the learning process and be continued at every opportunity.

Standing in chest-deep water, the learner leans forward and places the side of the face in the water so that the ear is submerged. He then inhales quickly through the mouth, rotates the head to the facedown position, and exhales. The breathing should be a continuous, rhythmic sequence. After the head has reached the facedown position, the learner starts exhaling while he rotates the head back to its original position. He is then ready for another breath and to repeat the cycle. This rhythmic breathing should be practiced first on one side and then on the other. The learner will soon determine which is his natural breathing side.

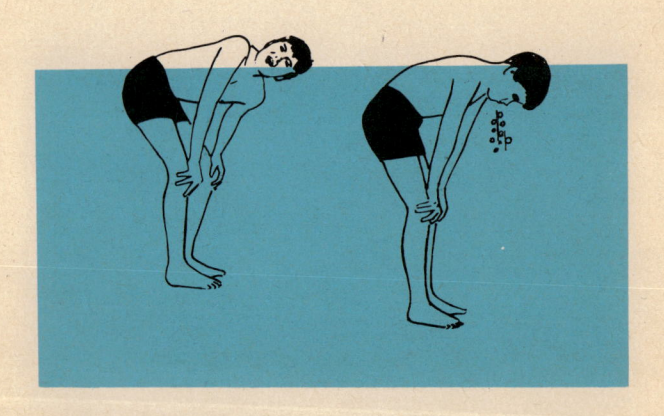

The aim is to get the learner to perfect the rhythmic breathing cycle until he can continue for 5, 10, 20, 30, 40, or even 50 times without stopping and still get adequate ventilation.

Rhythmic breathing can be practiced while doing kicking drills in a bracketed position, while kicking with one arm extended or with both arms at the side, or synchronized with arm action.

BUOYANCY AND BODY POSITION

Many of the skills that the learner has been practicing from the time of his first entry into the water have given him some feeling of the lifting effect of the water. The floating and body position skills should prove to the learner that water will support him with little or no effort.

The majority of beginners initially believe that it is necessary to stroke continually with the arms and legs to keep from sinking. Every effort should be made to dispel this belief. Success in this regard can be accomplished by constant emphasis and practice of breath control, relaxation, and body position. As soon as the learner experiences the effect of the body's natural buoyancy, he is ready to start adding the stroking movements that can result in moving through the water as opposed to the effort expended toward trying to prevent sinking.

Prone Float

Shallow water of a depth of from 2 to 2½ feet is ideal for learning the prone float. Lying extended in a prone position and supported by having his hands on the bottom, the learner takes a breath, places the face in the water, and slowly lifts the hands from the bottom and extends the arms in front of the head. If the toes are still on the bottom, a gentle push will usually raise them toward the surface, allowing the whole body to be suspended in a prone float position.

The prone float may also be taught by having the learner stand in chest-deep water with arms extended, take a breath, place face in the water, and gently push from the bottom or the side of the pool into a prone float position. Recovery is accomplished by drawing the knees under the body, pushing down with the arms, and, when the body has shifted from the horizontal to the vertical, straightening the legs, lifting the head, and coming to a standing position. Use of a partner helps the beginner to gain confidence in the initial learning stage. The slight push from the side or the bottom may help the less buoyant learner to achieve the feel of the prone floating position.

Jellyfish Float

This floating position can be helpful to the beginner in learning about the buoyant effect of the water and it also can be a basic starting skill for the prone float. Since the jellyfish float employs a facedown, relaxed, and suspended position, it is a fundamental skill for survival floating.

From a standing position in about chest-deep water, the learner bends forward and places the hands comfortably on the thighs. He then takes a breath and bends further forward so that the face is submerged and the hands are slid down close to the ankles. If all this is done slowly and in a relaxed manner, the feet will usually float free of the bottom, and the body will be floating with a portion of the rounded back showing above the water. As the skill is mastered, the arms and legs hang suspended and relaxed in this position. To regain footing, the learner slowly raises the head and upper body toward the surface, allowing the feet to settle on the bottom. Emphasis must be placed on moving slowly, and the learner should not attempt to stand until the feet are securely placed on the bottom and the body is balanced over them.

A partner or the instructor should be standing by during the learning process to help the beginner gain confidence and to assist him in standing if assistance should be needed.

To go from the jellyfish float to the prone float, the learner slowly raises the arms forward and extends the legs backward until the body is in a fully extended prone position. Recovery is accomplished by drawing the knees under the body, pushing down with the arms, and, when the body has shifted from the horizontal to the vertical, straightening the legs, lifting the head, and coming to a standing position. Continued practice will enable the learner to take a comfortable, balanced, and relaxed prone position that will be a standard position for all later strokes that are performed lying on the front. A partner or the instructor should be facing the learner during practice of this skill.

Back Float

This skill should be first attempted with either the instructor or a partner assisting. Standing in chest-deep water, the helper places his hands lightly under the learner's shoulder blades. The learner should submerge until the shoulders go just below the surface. Then he gently lies back in the water until the ears are submerged, arms are extended and relaxed along the sides, and the feet are extended. In many cases the heels will still be resting on the bottom, but most of the body weight will be supported by the water. Continued practice will enable the learner to perform this skill without the aid of his partner or instructor.

To assist the learner in recovering to the standing position, the partner can help by placing his hands at the learner's shoulder blades. The learner should drop the hips, bring the chin forward, draw the knees back, and let the arms reach backward and then scoop them forward. This maneuver will change the body position, enabling the learner to straighten the legs to the bottom and then finally to raise the head to regain the standing position.

The recovering to standing position can be described as that of a person reaching behind himself and pulling an imaginary armchair into position before attempting to straighten up and stand. The back float should be practiced until the learner can perform it unassisted in a relaxed and balanced position.

PROPULSION AND COORDINATED STROKING

Prone Glide

For an individual who has mastered the prone float position, initial propulsion consists simply of adding a push by the feet from the bottom or the side of the pool. A glide along the surface follows as the learner holds his breath, keeping the face in the water.

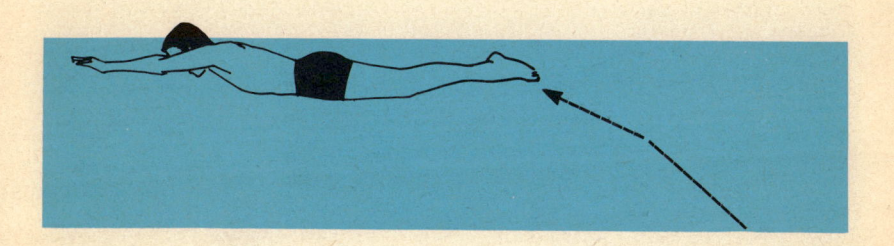

As momentum ends, the knees are brought up, the extended arms are pressed down, the legs are straightened to a position on the bottom, the head is now lifted, and the learner stands.

Continued practice, with emphasis on longer breath holding and a more vigorous pushoff, will result in a glide of several body lengths with ease. A facedown head position and a good streamlined body position should be continually emphasized in the practice sessions.

Prone Glide With Kick

Before adding the leg stroke to the prone glide, the learner should have practiced the crawl kick by using a variety of drills and learning practice situations. These drills can be practiced sitting or lying on the deck with legs extended over the pool, supported by a partner, bracketed against the overflow or a kicking rail, or using the support of a tube or a kickboard.

The initial kick recommended is the crawl kick, as described in detail in chapter 5. Learners will have an initial tendency to thrash up and down with bent knees, but continued corrections on straightening the legs and trying for relaxed ankles will help to overcome this. In correcting an extremely bent knee of a learner, the instructor should watch for the fault of keeping the legs stiff. Also, learners will sometimes tend to have a very narrow or shallow kick. This fault can be corrected by having the learner move the legs up and down so that the knees pass each other slightly. When enough coordination is established and some thrust has been developed, the kick can be added to the prone glide.

The kick glide is done by starting with the prone glide and adding the kick as soon as the gliding momentum is underway. Practice distance can be lengthened by the learner's adding rhythmic breathing, using a kickboard or an arm support. Without the use of an arm support, the kicking and breathing combination can be practiced by keeping both arms extended at the side or by keeping one arm extended and one arm at the side.

Back Glide

The learner starts this skill as if he were starting a back float. In chest-deep water, he submerges until the shoulders are in the water and then gently lies back, with chin tucked in slightly and arms extended and relaxed along the sides. He then gives an easy push against the bottom, which should give enough momentum to enable the body to glide a few feet along the surface of the water.

Many learners attempt to push too vigorously, thus causing water to wash over the face. There also is an initial tendency to bend at the hips. This bent position will interfere with the glide and cause the body to sink. Emphasis should be continually placed on a streamlined body position.

As practice continues, the learner will be able to thrust a little more vigorously against the bottom or from the side of the pool and gradually increase the length of the back glide. Recovery to the standing position is accomplished as in the back float.

Back Glide With Kick

Before adding the leg stroke to the back glide, the learner should have practiced kicking on the back by using a variety of drills and learning situations. The leg kick can be practiced from on the deck with legs extended over the side of the pool, with partner support, bracketed against the overflow or a kickrail, or using the support of a tube or a kickboard.

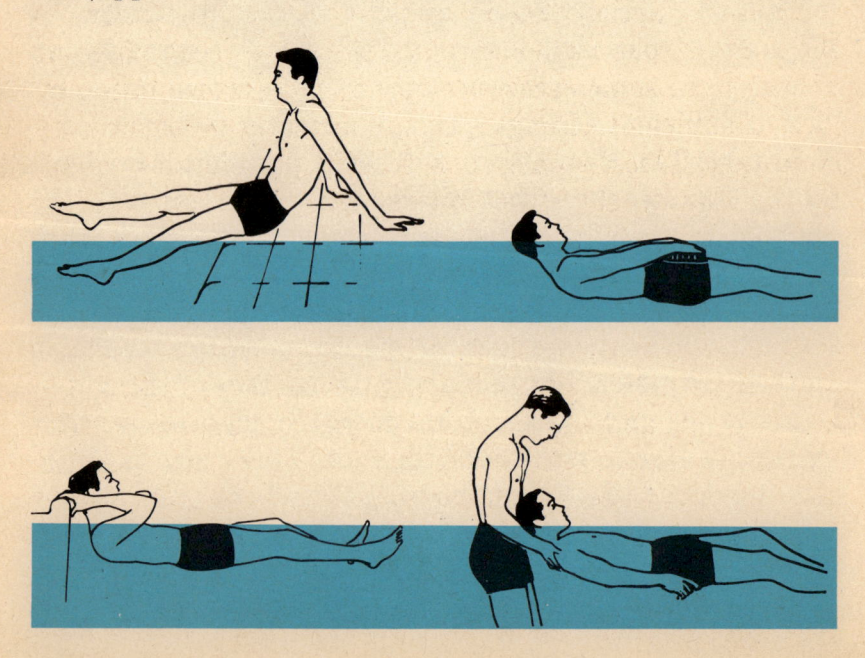

The kick is an alternate up and down action of the legs similar to the kick on the front. However, there is a little more bending of the knees, and the emphasis is on pressing the water up and backward on the upstroke, keeping the ankles relaxed. The tendency will initially be to kick too fast and hard, but this fault can be corrected by continually slowing down and trying to get the feel of the front of the foot pushing up and back against the water. This leg action is described in greater detail in chapter 5 in both the crawl and the back crawl analysis.

Starting with the back glide, the kick is initiated as soon as the body reaches the stretched-out glide position and while there is still momentum from the push. Since the face is out of water for ease of breathing, practice may be sustained for longer distances. The back glide with kick should be practiced until the learner achieves a well-balanced position, effective leg action, some endurance, and the ability to get back to standing position with ease.

Arm Stroke on the Front

The arm action recommended for most beginners is the crawl stroke movement with the arms recovering out of water. In some cases, because of poor coordination or lack of sufficient strength, the underwater recovery may be taught. This arm action is described in detail in chapter 5. For teaching beginners, the crawl stroke arm action can be simplified. The hand enters the water approximately in front of the shoulder and is angled downward. The hand pulls and presses backward near the center line of the body to about the thigh. Without pause, the arm is lifted with the shoulder, letting the elbow bend, and the hand stays behind the elbow. The shoulder carries most of the action as the arm recovers over the water and with the hand below and outside of the elbow. The hand then enters first about in front of the shoulder and, after being extended forward and downward, is ready to start the full cycle again.

Emphasis should be placed on ease and relaxation in the recovery and a slow pull and press through the water until the learner gets the feel of the movement.

The arm action can be practiced in standing-depth water, with the learner being supported by a partner or the instructor, using a leg support, or adding the arm action only to the prone glide. Initially, the action of the learner while standing can be practiced using one arm only. In order for the desired body position to be maintained, the face should be in the water, and initial practice then is limited to a normal breath-holding period.

Arm Stroke on the Back

The easiest arm action for the beginner to learn and coordinate on the back is called finning. The arms are fully extended along the sides, and the recovery is made by drawing the hands up along the sides to about the hip level. The fingertips are extended outward, and the hands are pressed backward toward the feet and then recovered, close to the body, to their original position. This pressing action, with both arms acting simultaneously, is a simple and natural movement and will tend to move the learner backward through the water. It can be practiced standing in chest-deep water, with partner support or with a flotation device. The finning action is then added to the back glide while there is still momentum from the push against the bottom or the side of the pool.

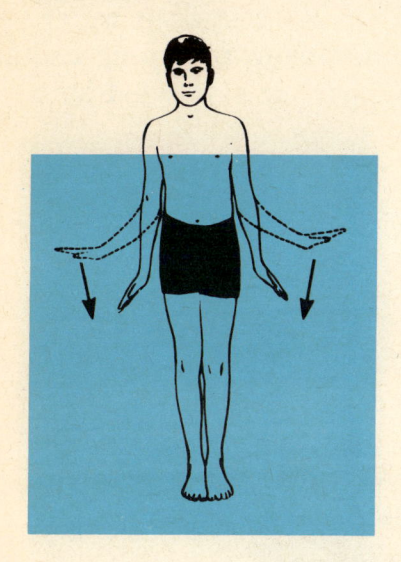

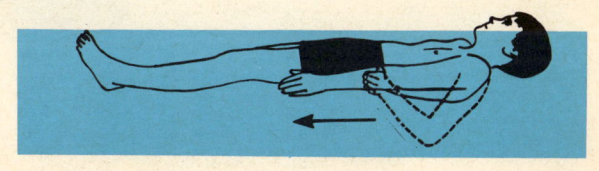

Some learners will tend to develop a semicircular sculling motion. Use of this motion can be encouraged since sculling is even more effective than the beginning finning movement.

Crawl Stroke for Beginners

Since the learner has achieved a balanced glide position and has learned and has been practicing separately the arm and leg movements, he is ready to combine them into a coordinated stroke.

The learner pushes off into a prone glide with the face in the water. He then should start an easy leg kick, as in the front kick glide, and then add the arm action. Initially, the combined stroke of arms and legs can be done for one full stroke, then two, and then a few strokes that can be practiced within the capacity of one breath. For continued practice, the learner can simply rotate the head, take another breath, and continue stroking.

Since practice of rhythmic breathing should have been a part of every practice session, this can now be added to the arm stroke while standing in chest-deep water. Another step might be the combination of breathing and arm stroke while using a leg support or supported by a partner or the instructor.

Coordination of breathing and arm stroke for the learner who breathes on the left is as follows: As the right hand angles forward and downward, the head is rotated to the left just enough for the mouth to clear the surface and allow inhalation through the mouth. Then the head is rotated so that the learner's face is back underwater facedown for exhalation.

Various combinations of coordination should be practiced. One might try these for example: From the prone glide, use arm movement and rhythmic breathing, with no leg action; from the prone glide, kick and add the rhythmic breathing, keeping the arms at the side. Kickboards and other flotation devices can be helpful at this stage to enable the learner to maintain a good working position and increase the amount of sustained practice.

Combined Stroke on the Back

From the back glide, the learner starts the leg action and then adds the finning movement of the arms. Since there is no breathing problem as long as correct head and body position is maintained, this beginner's stroke on the back is easily coordinated.

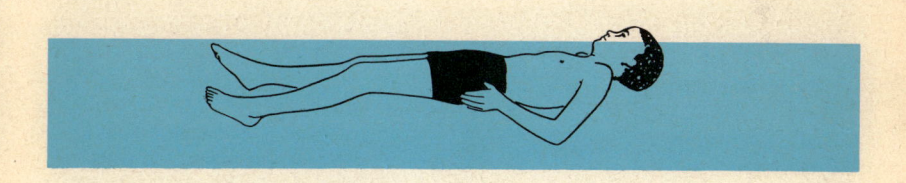

Continued emphasis should be on making all movements as easy and relaxed as possible so that the learner maintains a comfortable position and still makes some progress through the water. This is a valuable resting stroke for the beginner since it enables him to stay afloat, breathe freely, and move easily through the water, all with a minimum of effort.

PERSONAL SAFETY

Turning Over

When the learner can swim on both the front and the back, an important safety skill is the ability to change from one to the other position with ease.

To turn from the crawl stroke to the back position, the learner turns on the arm extended in front, drops the shoulder, and turns the head away from the shoulder while the other arm is drawn across the body and extended to the opposite side.

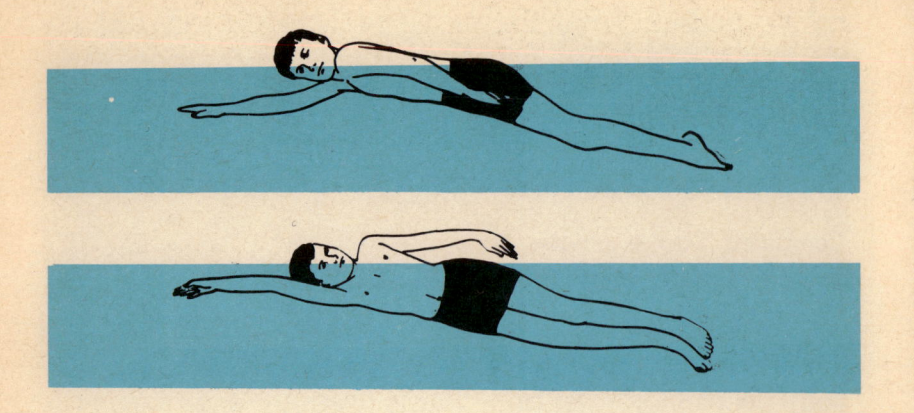

The turn from the back to the front position should be practiced as follows: If, for example, the learner wishes to turn to the left, he takes a breath, holds it, turns the head to the left, draws the right arm across the chest, and the body will rotate in the desired direction. As soon as the turn is completed, he continues stroking to maintain a horizontal body position and momentum.

Changing Direction

Changing direction is a simple but important safety skill for the beginner. While swimming, the learner reaches his forward arm in the direction that he wants to go and turns his head in the same direction. This action enables him to make a simple, wide turn. Continued practice will enable him to shorten the turn, which should be practiced in either direction. In the initial learning, emphasis should be placed on the legs' continuing to kick so as to maintain the horizontal position.

Treading Water

Treading water is a skill that enables the beginner to keep his face above the surface with the body in a vertical position. The ability to tread water and to go into either a prone or supine position from the vertical is an important survival safety skill.

With the arms outstretched just below the shoulder level, palms down and somewhat in front of the body, the hands move easily in wide circles, pressing slightly downward with the palms. For beginners, the crawl kick already learned can be used but it should be performed more slowly and slightly wider.

The body can be bent slightly forward at the trunk. The arm and leg action should be sufficient to keep the head just high enough so that the mouth and nose are out of water for ease of continued breathing.

Learners can practice using the legs only by holding lightly to the edge of the pool or while supported by a kickboard or flotation device. The arm action can be practiced separately in neck-deep water. Then, while holding on to the edge of the pool with one hand lightly, the learner can start the leg action and add the use of one arm. Finally, the skill can be practiced, still near a support or edge, with the use of both arms and legs. Continued practice should enable even beginning swimmers to keep themselves afloat in this vertical position easily for a short period.

As the learner progresses to using other leg strokes, the adjustment to treading water using a more efficient kick, such as a modified scissors or breaststroke kick, will be more easily accomplished.

ENTRIES

Getting into the horizontal position from the vertical is a safety skill that should be mastered before the learner is allowed to swim in deep water.

The skills involved can readily be learned by following a simple sequence of steps. First, standing in neck-deep water, the learner leans slightly forward and, with a minimum push against the bottom, swims to the horizontal and continues to shallower water.

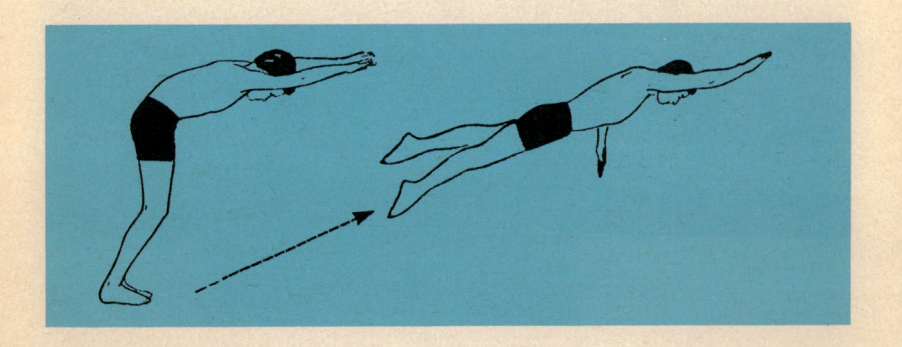

Next, under supervision, the learner swims out into deep water, stops kicking, allows his feet to sink until the body is in a vertical position, then swims to a horizontal position, and continues to the edge of the pool or to shallow water.

Finally, and still under supervision, the learner jumps from the deck into deep water and after his downward momentum stops he places the head between the extended arms, starts kicking, presses back alternately with the arms, and, upon reaching the surface, continues stroking to safety.

The progression for a beginner learning to dive is discussed in chapter 8.

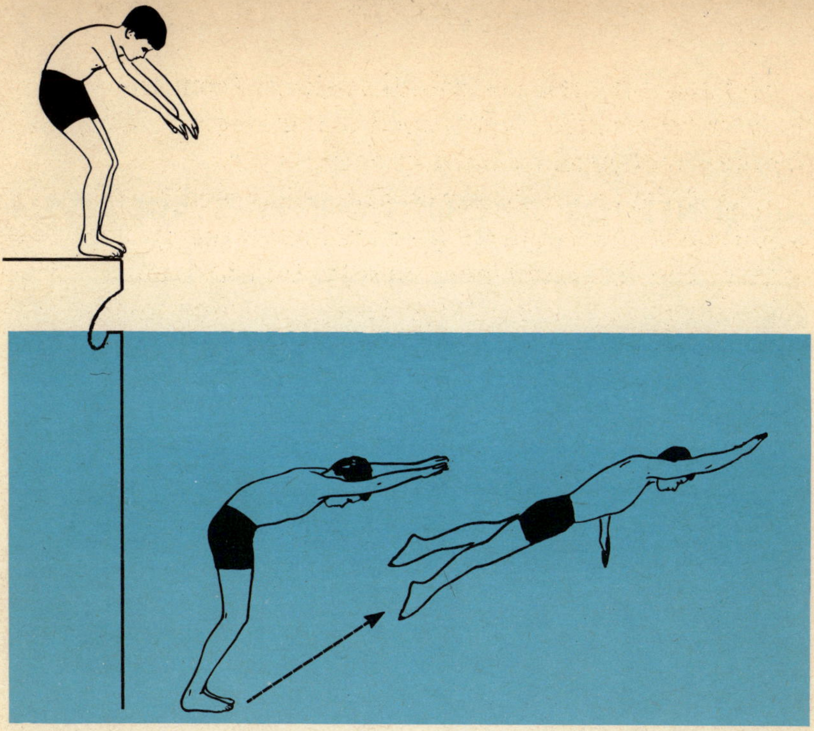

3

GUIDELINES FOR TEACHING DIFFERENT AGE LEVELS

Working With Preschool Children

In any work with preschool children (in this text the term "preschool" means "under six years old"), much of the success that can be achieved will depend upon the child's early experience with water. This experience actually started when the baby was first introduced to water when getting a bath.

The very young learn mostly through imitating and responding to certain sensations. In addition, the experience must be fun. Therefore, simple games become important in teaching this age group. For games to be effective it is usually better to work with at least two youngsters. Most games are intended for groups, and learning with a companion enhances the fun element.

Preschool children present special problems. They are not well coordinated and they cannot concentrate for more than a short time. Since they do not easily understand instructions and explanations, they need to be shown repeatedly.

Following are helpful suggestions to consider in teaching the very young.

1. The temperature of the water should be comfortable.
2. The children should be healthy, rested, and in a good frame of mind.
3. Never hurry progress or show impatience. Try to keep the youngster from getting an accidental noseful or faceful of water.
4. Keep the lessons short. Gauge the exact time to coincide with the interest and fun factor.
5. If group instruction is undertaken, a ratio of one aide to each child is recommended. One of the parents might be oriented to be the assisting adult.
6. Parent orientation is important. Help the parents to understand their role in, and responsibility for, supervising the preschool child in all his recreational aquatic activities, the limitation of swimming skills that the preschool child can acquire, and the aim and goals of the instructional program.

7. The use of any supports should be restricted to periods of instruction and supervised recreation. In recreational periods, if the wearing of artificial supports is allowed, the nonswimmers should be restricted to the shallow water area.

Working With Elementary School-Age Children

Most elementary school-age children take swimming instruction in organizational programs that are geared to offer instruction on a group basis. It is important therefore that children enrolled in such group instruction have developed a readiness and an acceptance for learning in a group situation.

To be successful, the instructor must gain the confidence of the group since this is inherent in instilling self-confidence in the individual.

In all group instruction, safety and supervision should be built in. A lifeguard or other responsible person should be situated in a lookout position while instructional classes are in progress since the instructor is not always located strategically to safeguard all the pupils.

Elementary school children in the 6-8-year-old bracket will usually make slower and more uneven progress than those who are 9 years of age or over. While progress in a class of elementary school-age children will therefore be uneven, the instructor should continue teaching at a pace that will keep the majority of the group active, interested, stimulated, and progressing.

It might be necessary to give extra attention to the slower learners by using aides when available. The class members who are making the quickest progress can be assigned extra work and practice to keep them satisfied. Each child needs to feel that he is an important member of the class, and all need constant encouragement regarding their progress. Since the progress of children in the 9-year-old-and-over bracket will be more even and steady, group instruction at this age level will usually result in a higher degree of success in completing beginner skills.

The following are additional teaching suggestions.
1. Keep instruction fun. Use of games and stunts will enhance the learning of required skills and keep the experience pleasurable.
2. Use terminology that is not associated with things children fear around the water; instead, liken skills and instructions on performance to things that children know and enjoy. For example, instead of saying "Put your face underwater," the instructor might say "Hide your face." The substitution of "Float like a log" for "Do a prone float" might give the children a better mental picture of what they are trying to do. Give skills familiar, exciting names; the object is to get the class to try and perfect the skills, not to have them know the technical names.
3. Keep the class busy and active. Be ready to change to a new skill or to practice another skill before they become restless and bored.
4. Do not make fun of, ridicule, or threaten the learner.

5. Demonstrate skills slowly and correctly. It may sometimes help to have a class member who is able to do a skill well perform the demonstration.
6. Most importantly, always provide for overall protection and supervision of the whole class.

Working With Teen-agers

Teen-agers present no special problems if they become motivated to learn how to swim. However, if an individual has reached this age level and is still a nonswimmer, the instructor should learn and understand the reasons and should make an earnest attempt to counteract them.

In some instances, being a nonswimmer at this age may have resulted solely from a lack of opportunity. On the other hand, some experience in the individual's background may be the cause. Fear of the water may be the result of a previous near-drowning experience or it may be an aftermath of simply viewing a water tragedy. Having heard a vivid account of a drowning tragedy or even repeated warnings from parents or other adults might be a contributing factor. The instructor may make some progress in dissipating these fears merely by bringing the causes out into the open. By firmly and clearly explaining the buoyancy of the body in the water, by outlining the ease and simplicity of swimming and stroking movements, by stressing relaxation, the instructor starts the process of building confidence.

It is important that the learner also has confidence in the instructor. The instructor builds this confidence by understanding the causes of the learner's fear, by never forcing the learner to attempt a skill until he is ready, and by always realizing that, until the adjustment process is complete, the fear is very real to the learner. Failure on the part of the pupil to successfully perform a simple skill should be met with encouragement, patience, and firm understanding, never with ridicule.

Nonswimmers in the teen-age group may attempt to avoid the opportunity to learn. Often this reluctance can be traced to social embarrassment and a fear of ridicule.

Instructors should attempt at every opportunity to motivate the teen-age nonswimmer or novice to become a swimmer by emphasizing the advantages. A skilled swimmer has a whole exciting world of recreational aquatic endeavors that he can enjoy. Such related activities as boating, sailing, water skiing, skin and scuba diving, and surfing can many times be the attraction that will motivate these young people to overcome their reluctance and emotional fears.

Working With Adults

Many adults have never learned to swim because of the lack of opportunity, and many will have developed fears and misconceptions that make learning to swim a problem. The same basic approach of building confidence, dissipating fears, and creating understanding that is explained in the preceding section on teen-agers will generally apply.

Adjustment, breath control, coordination, and relaxation will usually be the most difficult skills for the adult to master.

In many cases, early success in getting the adult to float and to make simple progress on the back will be helpful in instilling confidence and starting the process of relaxation.

The adult may be more successful in perfecting a simple side or breast stroke variant as opposed to the more difficult coordination necessary in the crawl stroke. The elementary backstroke should be included in the instruction since this is another simple means of propulsion and is a good resting stroke as well. The objective of all instruction for nonswimmer adults should be the development of sufficient skill to enable them to take care of themselves in deep water rather than the perfection of total performance.

Some adult beginners will want to learn the crawl stroke. In such cases, variations of the crawl such as the trudgen or the trudgen crawl may be the answer since these strokes can be more easily coordinated.

In a class of adults, progress will be uneven because of the many individual differences. Patience, encouragement, praise, and understanding will be necessary for success.

After the adult learns breath control and has become adjusted, proper artificial supports may be helpful in getting him to maintain a better working or practicing position. In this way, he should be able to continue to perform a series of practicing movements longer and thus speed up the learning process and help his coordination and stroking.

4

PHYSICAL LAWS GOVERNING BODY MOVEMENTS IN THE WATER

When individuals have mastered the skills in the beginner courses they are fairly safe swimmers and able to enjoy being in the water. At this point, different motivation approaches can be used to instill in the learner the desire to become a skilled swimmer. The instructor can point out the benefits and wide range of enjoyment open to the swimmer skilled in efficiently performing a variety of strokes and related skills.

Skilled swimmers are safe swimmers, and this alone justifies the necessary time and effort needed to become proficient in the water.

Swimming is fun. It is an ideal family sport since all ages can participate. However, to fully take advantage of the many facets of aquatic recreation requires proficiency in swimming and knowledge of water safety practices.

For most people, swimming is an excellent form of exercise for building and maintaining strength and vigor. In order, however, to derive the maximum benefit of swimming for fitness, the learner must have developed a degree of skill that will fully contribute to his mental and physical fitness.

Swimming for competition has a strong natural appeal. The tremendous increase of interest in age group competitive swimming and the growing popularity of synchronized swimming have created exciting areas of possible participation and enjoyment for the skilled swimmer.

For the individual to participate and fully enjoy the specialized sports of skin and scuba diving, water skiing, boating, and surfing, proficiency in swimming should be a prerequisite.

To progress from a beginning swimmer to a skilled swimmer, the individual should have not only an understanding of how the skills are performed but also some knowledge of the principles underlying the mechanics of the skills. These principles are really the physical laws that govern the actions of the body while in the water. Instructors certainly should have an understanding of these principles, and the learner, according to his age, training, and background, will make easier progress if he too understands them.

Buoyancy

Archimedes' Law states that a body submerged in a liquid (water) is buoyed up by a force equal to the weight of the liquid it displaces. Applying this law to swimming, the upward force that acts on the swimmer is equal to the weight of the volume of water that is identical with the volume of the submerged portion of the swimmer's body. If this buoyant force is proportional to the amount of displaced water, the volume or size of the swimmer is significant in his ability to float. One of the main factors in buoyancy depends on the ratio between weight and volume. Other factors will be breath control, balanced center of gravity, relaxation, and knowledge of how to perform the skill.

SPECIFIC GRAVITY

This is the ratio between the weight of the human body and the weight of an equal body of water. Since the specific gravity of water is 1.0, a body will float when it has a specific gravity of less than 1.0. When the body displaces a weight of water greater than its own weight, that body will float.

The degree of buoyancy will depend a great deal on body type. Since bone and muscle have a higher specific gravity than does adipose tissue (fat), big-boned, muscular individuals would tend to have a higher specific gravity, resulting in negative buoyancy, and would therefore sink.

BALANCE AND CENTER OF BUOYANCY

On land, the body rotates around its center of gravity, which is approximately the hip region. In water, the body rotates around its center of buoyancy or fulcrum, which is the chest region. The reason for this is that since the chest contains the lungs and when filled with air is light for its size it becomes the most buoyant area of the body.

The legs, because of a high percentage of bone and muscle, have a high specific gravity and will usually sink. Another reason is the longer distance of this end of the lever, that is, the distance from the toes to the chest or fulcrum. This causes the body to be overbalanced at the leg end. In cases where the lower extremities have a lower specific gravity (greater adipose tissue) and displace a volume of water that weighs as much or more than they weigh, the center of buoyancy will tend to move down from the chest region. When the center of buoyancy moves down to a point that coincides with the center of gravity, the body is balanced perfectly and the swimmer will float in a horizontal position.

It can readily be understood, therefore, why the jellyfish float position is the most buoyant position that the body can assume in the water. The head is in the water and all the segments of the body are as close as possible to the center of buoyancy (chest) so that when the lungs are filled with air, most people will float. This is the simplest test for determining whether a person has enough buoyancy to learn to float motionless on the back.

FLOATING MOTIONLESS

To successfully float motionless, the majority of persons will find a balanced position somewhere between the vertical and the horizontal. To find individual balance, most swimmers will need to experiment with redistributing the body weight around the center of buoyancy. For instance, having the arms in the water to an extended position directly above the head results in lengthening and adding weight to the upper part of the body and will cause a counterbalancing effect to the heavier legs. Raising the upturned hands out of water adds further weight at this end, resulting in added balance, and will also tend to raise the legs. Both of these actions cause the center of gravity to come up closer to the center of buoyancy.

The lower portion of the body can be shortened by flexing the knees, which action will also tend to raise the center of gravity closer to the center of buoyancy. With the head back and the back arched, the result will be some further expanding of the chest, which will help vital breathing capacity and greater displacement of water. Slim, light-boned individuals and large persons with an excess of adipose tissue would have a lower specific gravity and would float with greater ease than the average individual.

The person with negative buoyancy can be compared to a lead weight and would sink since there is relatively small displacement with great weight. The individual with positive buoyancy can be compared to an inflated balloon since there would be a relatively large displacement of water with comparatively little weight.

BREATH CONTROL AND VITAL CAPACITY

The maximum volume of air taken in by a swimmer in one inhalation is called vital capacity. Filling the lungs increases buoyancy or lowers the specific gravity since it increases the body volume without increasing the weight. This is the reason why many swimmers can float only when their lungs are full of air. A person with air-filled lungs can be compared to a person wearing a life jacket since he has increased volume without any appreciable increase in weight. Breath control is important since many swimmers will float motionless only when their lungs are full and they are properly balanced. Maximum volume can be maintained by periods of breath holding followed by rapid expiration and inspiration.

Since most individuals will not be successful in floating in a horizontal position, a common error is for learners to start in the horizontal position. The result will usually be that the legs start to sink. As they sink, momentum increases and causes the individual to be pulled under the surface. It is preferable for the learner to start in a vertical position and then gently arch the back, extend the arms, and assume the floating position. In this way, the legs should lift to the point of balance according to the buoyancy of that individual if the principles outlined have been followed.

Motion

An understanding of how Newton's three laws of motion apply to human motion while in the water should lead to a better understanding of the mechanics of effective stroking.

LAW OF INERTIA

The law of inertia states that a body remains at rest or in uniform motion in a straight line unless acted upon by some external force. Application of this law to swimming means that two types of inertia are involved: resting or stationary inertia and moving inertia. When the swimmer's body is in motion it possesses moving inertia and will have a tendency to keep on moving. Thus, momentum is created. If the body stops moving, either by the swimmer's action or by having the outside resistance of air and water overcome the moving inertia, the body then possesses resting, or stationary, inertia. When this happens, it takes conscious force to get the body moving again. It is obvious, therefore, that it is more efficient to keep momentum going than to progress in constant starts and stops. This law also has some distinct implications for the strokes that traditionally result in a long glide. When the aim of the swimmer is to get from one spot to another as fast as possible, top efficiency is of utmost importance. In such cases (competition or approaching a victim in a water rescue), a swimmer doing a breaststroke would de-emphasize the glide. If he is swimming for pleasure, survival, or self-rescue, a moderate glide should be used but it should never be held so long that forward momentum is completely lost. In these cases, even though more effort may be expended by the inertial lags, the more relaxed movement and period of time involved counterbalance the lessening of efficiency.

LAW OF ACCELERATION

The law of acceleration states that the rate of change of momentum of a body is proportional to the force applied, and occurs in the direction in which that force acts. Applying this law to efficient stroking movements means that force should be applied in a way that the action will take place parallel to the line of propulsion. As an example, in the crawl stroke arm action the hand should be moved as parallel to the midline of the body as is possible without unnecessary muscular tension.

LAW OF ACTION AND REACTION

The law of action and reaction states that every action has an equal and opposite reaction. Applying this law to stroking means that, if the swimmer wishes to move forward, he must push the water backwards. The most efficient propulsive action should be made in a direction opposite to the line of travel. Movements that press the water upward, to the side, or downward do not contribute to forward progress and should be held to a minimum or eliminated when possible. As an example, in the arm action of the sidestroke the pull of the lower arm should be horizontal rather than vertical. This law when applied to the crawl stroke arm action can help a swimmer understand why the catch should not occur by placing the hand on the surface of the water. If the catch is made at the surface, the initial action would be almost directly downward and the reaction therefore would be upward, not contributing anything to forward motion.

Leverage

In stroking, the entire arm and hand acts as a third-class lever. Force is applied between the fulcrum (shoulder joint) and the resistance of water to the surface of the arm and hand. The law of levers states that the product of the force, times the length of the force arm, is equal to the product of the resistance, times the length of the resistance arm.

The *force* is the muscle force applied; the *force arm* is the distance from the shoulder joint to the point where the force is applied (about 2 inches from the shoulder joint where the muscles involved are inserted); *resistance* is mostly water resistance, and the *resistance arm* is the distance from the hand back to the fulcrum.

Flexing the elbow as the arm moves through the water shortens the resistance arm, with the result that the same propulsive effort can be effected with only about half the force applied compared to when the arm is straight.

Since water is denser than air it offers the greater resistance to movement. While resistance handicaps forward motion it is also the factor that enables the swimmer to propel himself. The swimmer can minimize resistance in several ways. He can improve the body position, eliminate actions that cause the body to move from side to side, and minimize negative actions.

The best body position is one in which the swimmer presents the smallest possible surface against the direction of travel. Keeping the body as level and streamlined as possible cuts down resistance. For instance, if the legs are allowed to drop, the body presents more surface against the line of travel, and resistance increases. Eliminate incorrect movements that cause the swimmer to move from side to side since they also increase resistance.

Recovery movements of arms and legs actually oppose forward motion. They tend to push against the water in the line of travel and thereby slow forward progress. Since air has much less resistance than water, strokes in which the arms can be recovered out of water are the more efficient. Leg strokes that can be executed and recovered as much as possible in line with the trunk of the body will be the more efficient also.

Relaxation

No swimmer attempting to propel himself is ever completely relaxed. The aim of the skilled swimmer is the relaxation of those muscles that are not contributing to the particular movement. Activating muscles that are not being used in a stroke can actually inhibit the desired movement, as well as hasten fatigue. The actions and movements of beginners in the water are usually awkward, tense, and tiring since they use many more muscle groups than necessary.

Breathing

The importance of proper breathing and breath control cannot be overemphasized. Any person attempting to swim efficiently while not getting a sufficient and regular supply of oxygen will soon tire. The art of rhythmic breathing can be learned and perfected if constantly practiced from the very beginning stage.

In all strokes, inhalation and exhalation (the act of breathing) must be done in a manner that will result in minimum interference with stroking rhythm and minimize the change in body position.

Proper breathing techniques are also important for health reasons since incorrect techniques can contribute to ear and sinus infections. The respiratory muscles must maintain an air pressure equal to or greater than the inward pressure of the water if water is to be prevented from entering the nose. Air should be exhaled mostly through the mouth and some through the nose since this practice will also prevent the entry of water into the nasal passages.

In the strokes where the face is carried beneath the surface, the interval when air is inhaled should be short; therefore, air should be inhaled quickly through the mouth. Exhalation is begun through the mouth and nose as soon as the head returns to its normal position. If some air remains before inhaling again, it should be expelled through the mouth just as the mouth clears the water.

Some skilled swimmers who possess good breath control do not exhale until just before they are ready to take another breath, at which time they expel the air through both the nose and mouth. This is referred to as explosive breathing and does prolong the period of greater buoyancy.

The swimmer is striving to breath at regular intervals, minimize interference with stroking mechanics, and maintain sufficient breath control to prevent ear and sinus infection.

Other Factors To Be Considered

The degree of skill that the swimmer can develop will depend upon his physical endowments, practice and conditioning, and the mental factors involved. In order to improve skill efficiency, the instructor and the swimmer should understand the necessity for adapting the basic principles of effective stroking to the physical endowments of the individual. The chapters on stroking mechanics should be interpreted as basic information, but understanding the principles will dictate that structural differences of swimmers necessitate modification of stroking mechanics. There is no way of performing a style of swimming that is best for all individuals. Swimmers and instructors who do not understand the applicable principles and physical laws will many times copy the "peculiar" style of an outstanding swimmer without realizing that such a style may simply be an adaptation of stroking mechanics and principles that best suited that individual swimmer's physical endowments.

5

ANALYSIS OF BASIC SWIMMING STROKES

Sidestroke

The sidestroke is relatively simple and easy to learn. The head is carried in a position that facilitates free breathing. It is favored by many instructors as a good coordinated stroke for adults to learn. The kick used is important as a basic leg action in lifesaving carries and has additional usage in the sidestroke variants, underwater swimming, treading water, and survival swimming. The action of the lower arm is also important when learning lifesaving carries.

BODY POSITION

The body lies in a side horizontal position with the back flat. The legs are fully extended, with toes trailing and comfortably pointed, legs together. The head is cradled against the water, aligned with the body, and is rotated just enough so that the nose and mouth are clear of the water.

In the glide position, the lower arm is fully extended below the surface and beyond the head. The upper arm is extended along the side, with the hand at the thigh.

ARM ACTION

During the glide the lower arm is extended palm downward, and the swimmer is riding on this extended arm. To start the positive action, he flexes the elbow so that the palm and inside of the arm start pressing backward almost directly toward the feet. As the arm and hand have pressed back to a point just past the shoulder, the palm continues to press back, with the elbow staying fairly close to the body. In a smooth, easy, and continuous motion the arm is kept close to the body, with the hand, palm down, leading the elbow and arm to the original extended position.

The upper arm is recovered from its extended position at the thigh by drawing the hand to a point approximately in front of the shoulder. In the recovery, the arm is kept close to the body to minimize resistance. The wrist is slightly flexed in a position that allows the hand to then press almost directly backward and downward as the elbow extends, bringing the arm to the position at the thigh.

LEG ACTION

The action described is called a scissors kick. From the extended position, with both legs together and in line with the body, the recovery is started by flexing the hips, knees, and ankles, keeping the heels in line with the back.

Next, the legs are separated in a flexed position, with the top leg extending laterally forward with ankle hooked and the lower leg moving to a position about three-quarters extended to the rear. Without stopping, both legs start the positive action by pressing backward and finally inward to the centerline.

The calf of the top leg presses backward and then finishes as the ankle extends to the centerline. The lower leg straightens at the knee as the instep presses vigorously backward and inward. Both legs start the positive action simultaneously, with the legs ending together and fully extended for the glide position.

BREATHING

The recommended technique calls for the swimmer to exhale as the top arm and the legs are going through their positive actions. If the proper head position is maintained, free breathing during the entire stroking movement will result.

COORDINATION

Since the movement of the top arm and that of the legs coincide in both the recovery and positive action, this is the key to coordinating the stroke. The lower or extended arm starts and goes through the positive action while the top arm and legs recover. A moderate glide follows but should not be prolonged to a point where forward momentum is lost.

Sidestroke

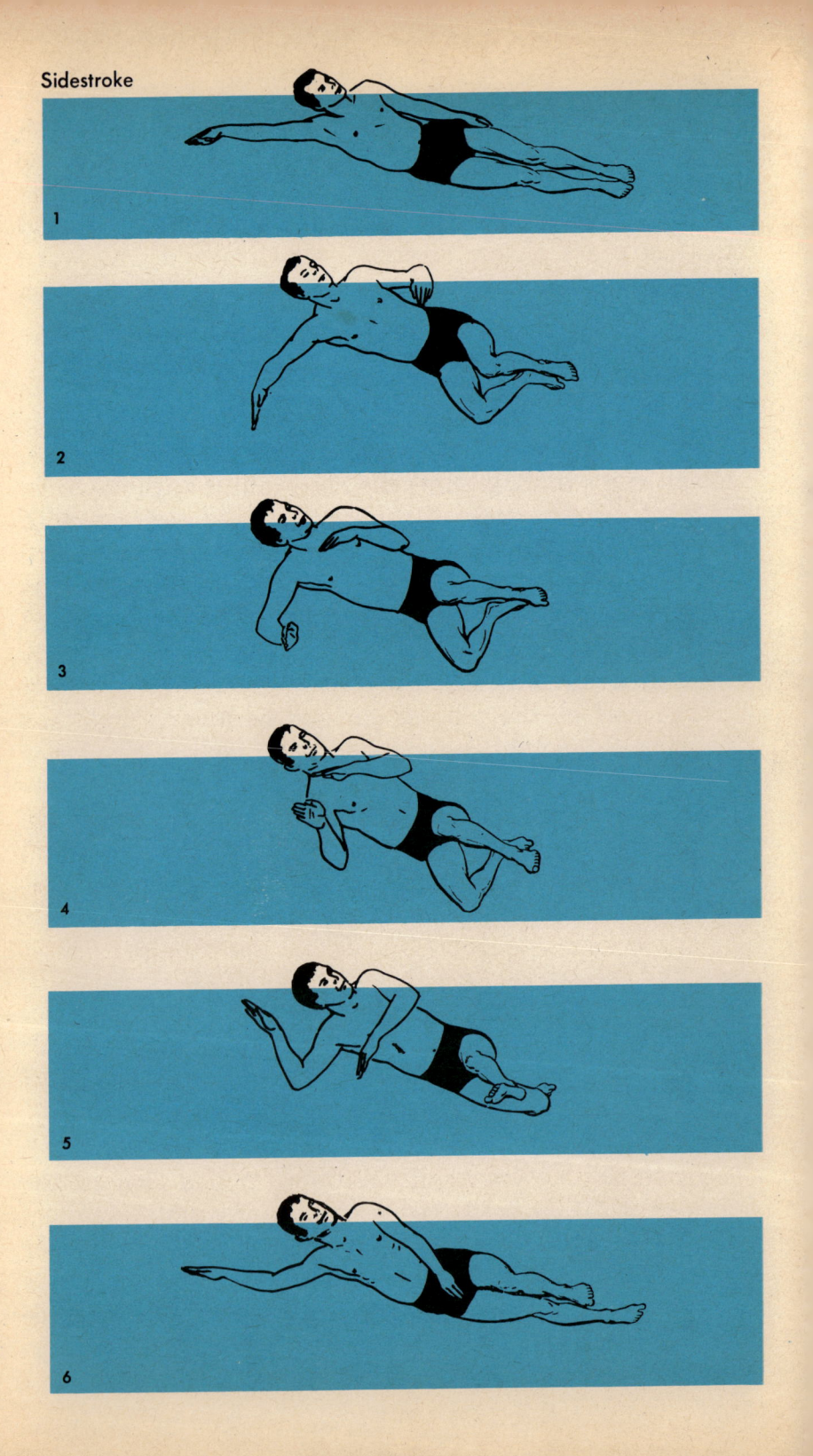

1

2

3

4

5

6

Elementary Backstroke

The elementary backstroke is primarily a resting or survival stroke. Since it requires little effort and permits easy and uninterrupted breathing, it can be used whenever the swimmer wants to recover from strenuous effort and still make some moderate progress through the water. It employs a relaxed, paired movement and is easy to learn. The kick, if done properly, can be useful in some lifesaving skills.

BODY POSITION

The body is in a supine horizontal position and is submerged except for the head. The head is submerged to about the level of the ears, thus leaving the face completely out of water with no hindrance to normal inhalation and exhalation. The back should be almost flat, with the legs and hips slanted down slightly lower than the head and shoulders. All arm and leg action is performed beneath the surface of the water. The arms are extended at the side, palms touching the thigh, and the legs are fully extended and trailing.

ARM ACTION

From the glide position, the hands are drawn slowly along the sides by flexing the elbows, and the hands and elbows remain close to the body throughout this movement in order to cut down resistance. When the hands have reached a position just below the shoulders, they are fully extended, still below the surface, to a point slightly above shoulder level. At this extended position, the fingers are pointed outward, palms facing backward, and the arms are ready for the start of the propulsive phase. The palms and inside of the arms then press simultaneously back toward the feet in a broad, sweeping movement until the hands return to the extended position at the thighs. The arms are now in the glide position of the stroke.

LEG ACTION

In the starting or gliding position, the legs are together, fully extended. The recovery is started by flexing the knees and ankles so that the heels drop down and move back toward the hips. The thighs should be kept fairly straight and in line with the body. When the heels have dropped to directly below the knees, the feet are rotated so that the toes are pointing to the side. During this action, the knees will spread slightly and the feet are rotated to a position outside the knees. At this point, the feet are spread wider than the knees.

The recovery action should be made slowly and easily to lessen resistance. At this stage, the legs are in a position for the positive action. Without pause, the thrust is made by pressing backward and upward as the inside of the lower leg and foot is pressing back against the water. The legs finish the full extension until the feet are back into the glide position, with toes pointed. The entire leg action is performed in one continuous and flowing movement that ends with the legs coming together in the extended position, with toes pointed.

BREATHING

Since the face is out of the water during the entire stroke, breathing presents no problem. It is still advisable to coordinate breathing at regular intervals by taking one breath for each complete stroke cycle. Inhalation occurs during the recovery and exhalation during the positive action of the arms and legs.

COORDINATION

With the swimmer in the glide position, legs extended and arms at the side, the recovery of the arms is started. When the hands have been drawn to about the waist, the legs start to recover. When the arms and legs are fully recovered, the positive action of both is simultaneous.

The arm and leg action ends with the body in the extended and streamlined glide position. The length of the glide will vary, but since the recovery of the arms and legs underwater causes much resistance, the recovery for the next stroke should start while there is still momentum so that it will not be completely lost as a result of this negative action.

Elementary Backstroke

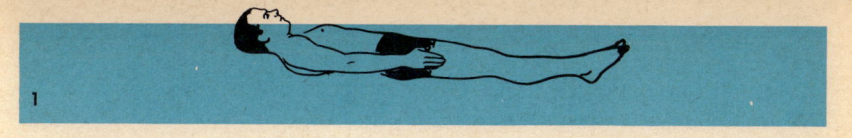

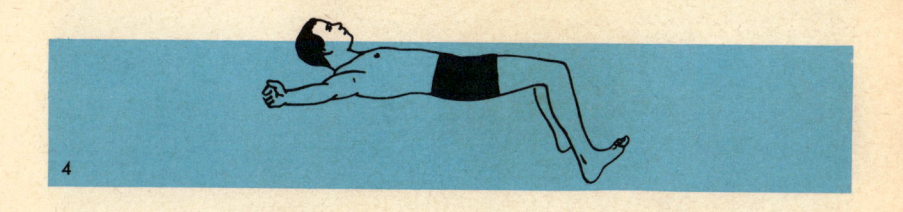

Breaststroke

The breaststroke is one of the oldest forms of propulsion and for many centuries was considered the best stroke to be taught to nonswimmers. Today it is one of the four strokes used in competition. It is a very useful stroke in lifesaving and survival swimming. Performed effectively, and with slight variation, it is a good stroke to use in approaching a victim since it enables the rescuer to have optimum vision and is reasonably fast. The kick can be modified for use in many rescue situations.

BODY POSITION (STARTING AND GLIDING)

The body should be maintained in a streamlined prone horizontal position, with the back flat. Arms are extended in front of the head with hands together and palms down and slanted slightly downward. Legs are extended with the hips and feet just below the surface. The head is positioned so that the water is about at eyebrow level.

ARM ACTION

From the starting position, the action begins by pressing the palms diagonally downward to just outside the shoulder line. With elbows high, the arms press almost directly backward in a continuous movement, with the palms not going beyond the elbows. During this action, the palms and inside of the arms press back toward the feet. During the last part of the arm action, the hands are brought fairly close together in a rounded motion and lead the elbows in the recovery to the extended position, palms down and slanting slightly downward.

LEG ACTION

The legs are together and fully extended in line with the trunk and just below the surface. The recovery starts by drawing the heels, which are slightly apart, toward the trunk and just below the surface. When the heels have been drawn to a point almost over the knees, the feet are rotated so that the ankles are hooked and toes are pointing to the side. During this action, the knees will spread slightly and the feet are rotated to a position outside the knees.

Without pause, the hips, knees, and ankles are extended, thus bringing the feet a little outward and backward through an arc. In this backward action, the sole, instep, and inside of the calf will be pressing almost directly backward against the water, and the resulting pressure against the water provides the major propelling force. The kick finishes with the extension of the ankles into a streamlined position.

The amount of rotation of the thigh will widen or narrow the arc of the backward kick. The important aspect in developing power is the emphasis on the pressing as directly backward as possible and not the width of the kick.

Since water is virtually incompressible, a breaststroke kick that emphasizes the squeeze is not effective. Squeezing of the legs together simply causes water to swirl about the legs and results in only a small force being directed backward.

BREATHING

The swimmer inhales through the mouth during the positive action of the arms by hyperextending the neck so that the head lifts just high enough for the mouth to clear the surface. The head is then dropped back to the starting position, and exhalation occurs during the extension and glide.

COORDINATION

The arms start the action, and the legs start to recover as the arms are pressing through the last part of the positive action. The legs kick as the arms are recovered to their extended position. A moderate glide follows but should not be prolonged to a point where forward momentum is lost.

Breaststroke

1

2

3

4

5

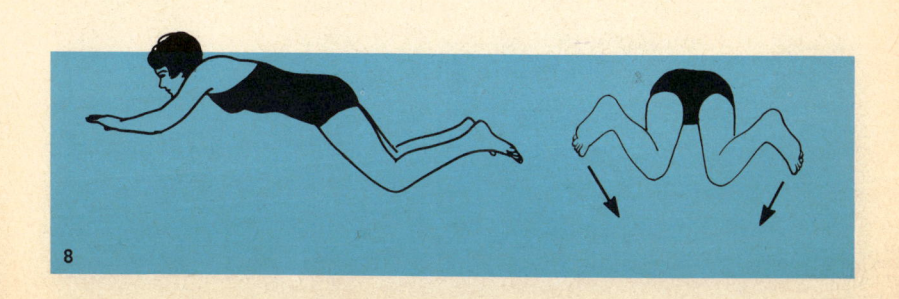

6

7

8

Crawl Stroke

Ability to perform an effective crawl is a mark of the skilled swimmer. Actually, the crawl is not only the fastest stroke but is extremely efficient. Since the kick is performed in line with the long axis of the body and the arms are recovered over the water, there is minimum resistance in the recovery or negative movements. The prone position enables a continuous application of well-applied force of the arms that is almost directly backward, which also adds to the smooth and efficient total stroke. Ability to perform an efficient crawl is useful in lifesaving when it is necessary to get quickly to a victim in danger.

The stroke mechanics described are the 6-beat crawl, but, as mentioned previously, structural differences will many times dictate some modification of stroking movements.

BODY POSITION

The swimmer is in a prone horizontal position with body flat. The head is aligned with the body, with the waterline approximately at the middle of the forehead, but this position may be adjusted slightly up or down to compensate for differences in body bouyancy. The arms and legs are extended.

ARM ACTION

At the entry, the fingers lead as the hand enters the water approximately in front of the shoulder. The arm is angled forward and downward, and the catch is made by flexing the wrist slightly, which positions the palm so that it faces almost directly backward. Without pause, the hand presses backward near the centerline of the body as the elbow bends.

As the hand passes the midpoint under the body, the palm continues to face and push backward, and the elbow draws closer to the trunk. As the hand pushes away from the trunk, it is swung upward out of the water as a continuation of the momentum established in the pushing-back or rounding-off action. The action should not continue to a position where the palm presses upward toward the surface.

When the arm is pressed back to a point just below and in front of the shoulders, the wrist is extended and at this point there is maximum flexing of the elbow. It is at this midpoint that maximum efficiency of the press (arm action) exists since almost all of the force is directed entirely backward.

The recovery is initiated by using the momentum from the end of the propulsive phase of the arm action. The emphasis should be on a free-swinging and relaxed recovery that is effected from the shoulder. An easy, rolling motion of the upper trunk will facilitate the recovery. The lower arm and hand will be relaxed until just prior to the entry as the arm is recovered loosely forward from the shoulder. If the recovery arm is swung low and wide, the hips, legs, and shoulders will shift out of alignment, thus causing a side-to-side movement that would be resistant to forward progress. As the swimmer leans into the water on the propelling arm, the shoulder of the recovering arm will be lifted, thus making the recovery over the surface easier.

It should be understood that many variants of the arm action described are acceptable. Length of arm, amount of roll, and elbow flexion will cause variations in the propelling action. Constant practice and experimentation will enable the swimmer to develop an efficient crawl stroke if the necessary variations do not violate the principles of good stroke mechanics. Some degree of roll about the long axis of the body is essential to developing a coordinated arm action in the crawl.

LEG ACTION

The action of the leg is commonly called a flutter kick, which is an alternating up and down action of the legs. The kick originates from the hip and is an undulating action of the lower leg, ankle, and foot. The knee and the ankle remain relaxed throughout. Flexibility of the ankles and feet will increase the kick's effectiveness. This is shown when swim fins are used in the crawl kick since the greatly increased flexibility of the fins, as well as their greater size, adds much to effective forward motion.

In the crawl kicking action, a relaxed ankle and foot will naturally produce a toeing-in effect. The toeing-in results from the anatomical structure of the ankle and the foot, the water pressure, and the desired relaxation. The swimmer therefore should not consciously attempt to toe-in since to do so would negate the necessary and desired relaxation.

The kick contributes to forward progress but serves mainly to balance and stabilize the effects of the swinging motion of the arms and the rolling of the body.

Propulsion is established by the alternate action of one leg moving down as the other moves up. Generally, the kick will be in a vertical plane, but effective variations resulting from the body roll can still provide the necessary balance and stability. Overkicking will simply lead to fatigue and retard the effectiveness of the overall stroke.

Crawl Stroke

3

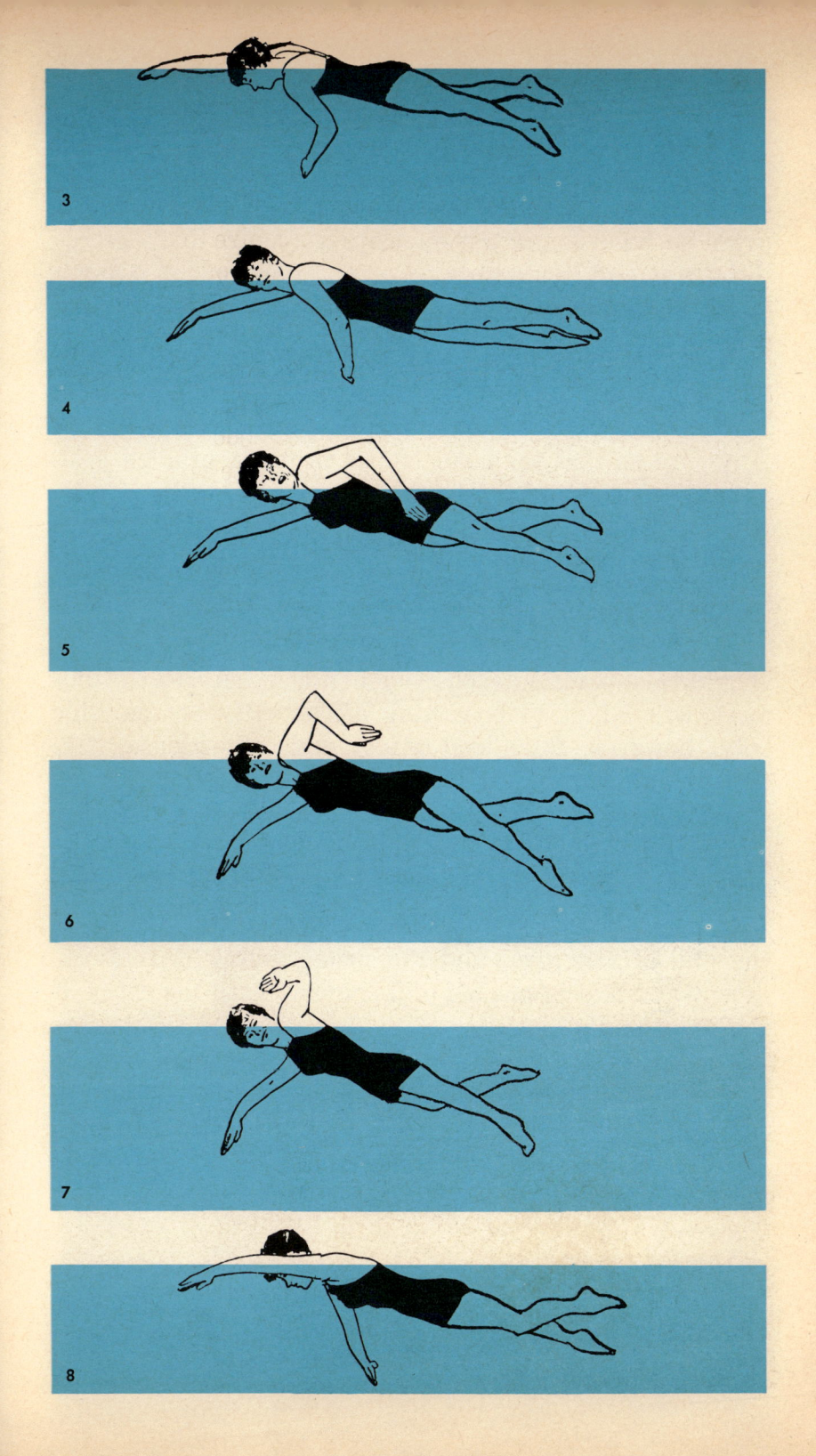

4

5

6

7

8

65

BREATHING

Inhalation is effected as the head is rotated just enough to bring the mouth to the surface. It should occur as the arm on the breathing side is starting the last half of the press backward and the opposite arm has just entered the water and is starting to extend downward. After a quick inhalation through the mouth, exhalation is done more slowly through both the mouth and nose and should finish just as the head again is rotated and the mouth clears the surface.

Assuming that the head is in a properly cradled position and depending on the swimmer's speed, the inhalation can actually take place with the mouth below surface level, in a trough of air that is created by the flow of water about the head.

A complete breathing cycle, inhalation and exhalation, should take place on each cycle of the arms. Most swimmers will adapt to breathing consistently on one side only; however, for added safety and convenience, it is desirable for swimmers to learn to breathe on either side.

COORDINATION

In a 6-beat crawl, there are three downward beats to the pull of one arm, and the usual timing is that the downward beat of one leg will coincide with the entry of the arm on the opposite side. As explained in the leg action description, since the kick serves to give balance and stability, overkicking should be avoided. The best coordination of arms, legs, and breathing is that which develops as a natural response of the individual swimmer. Good coordination should result in a forward motion that is smooth and constant.

Back Crawl

The back crawl is the most efficient stroke performed on the back and is one of the four strokes used in competition. Since the face is clear of the water, free breathing is easy; therefore when the arms and legs are properly coordinated, this style of swimming can be useful in swimming practically any distance. Even though this stroke has very little use in lifesaving it is classified as a style that skilled swimmers should be able to perform efficiently.

BODY POSITION

The body should be on the back, in a horizontal position, with the head aligned with the spine and submerged to about the level of the ears. The back is kept as straight or flat as possible. The hips should be just below the surface and the legs fully extended.

ARM ACTION

The hand enters the water, little finger leading, in line with the shoulder, with the arm kept straight but not rigid. In order to move the hand to a position about 12 inches deep in preparation for the positive action, the swimmer rolls slightly on the long axis of the body with the hand pressing to make the catch. The arm then sweeps outward and backward until approximately at the shoulder level. At this point, flexion begins in the elbow, and the hand pushes and then rotates so that the palm finally pushes downward at full extension. This will lift the shoulder nearer the surface and will facilitate arm recovery. The recovery is initiated by this lifting of the shoulders, allowing the arm to follow almost perpendicular to the surface and back to the point of entry.

LEG ACTION

The kick is similar to the crawl kick on the front in that it is an alternate up and down action of the legs originating from the hip, with flexion and relaxation occurring at the knees and ankles. On the upward kick, there is greater flexion at the knee, which will allow the upper surface of the lower leg and the foot to apply maximum force backward to the line of travel.

Overkicking should be avoided since it will only cause undue fatigue. Greater flexibility in the foot and ankle will add to the backward propulsive force.

BREATHING

Since the face should be clear of the water at all times, free breathing poses no difficulty. However, a regular cycle of inhalation through the mouth and exhalation through the nose and mouth should be maintained on every complete cycle of the arms.

COORDINATION

Arm and leg coordination is achieved by developing a regular stroking rhythm. For a regular 6-beat back crawl, there will be three upward beats for each arm action. One arm moves upward in the recovery at the same time as the opposite leg is kicking upward.

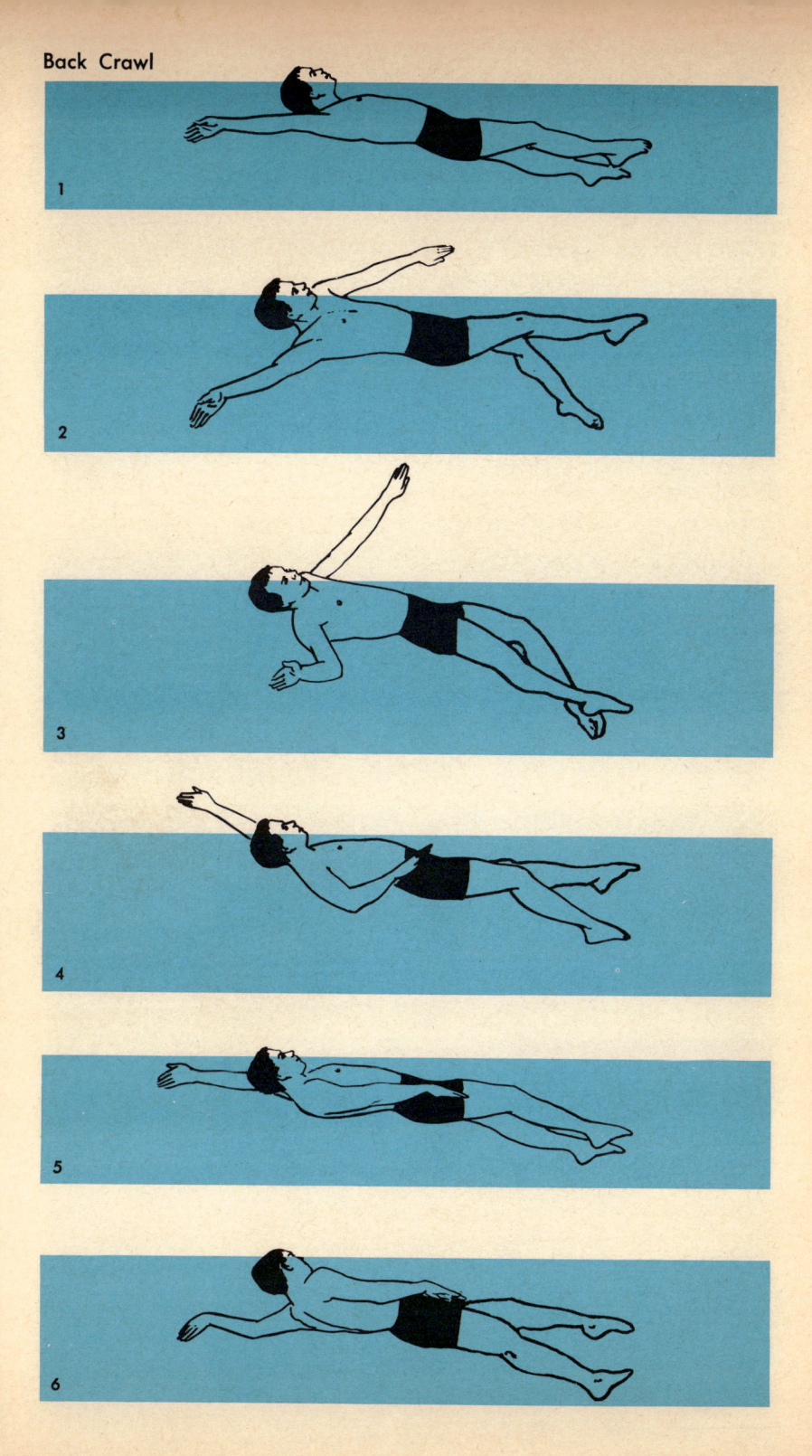

Back Crawl

1

2

3

4

5

6

69

ADDITIONAL STROKES AND VARIATIONS

Overarm Sidestroke

This variation of the sidestroke enables the swimmer to recover the top arm out of the water, thus increasing the efficiency of the stroke by minimizing the resistance in the recovery or negative phase of the arm movement.

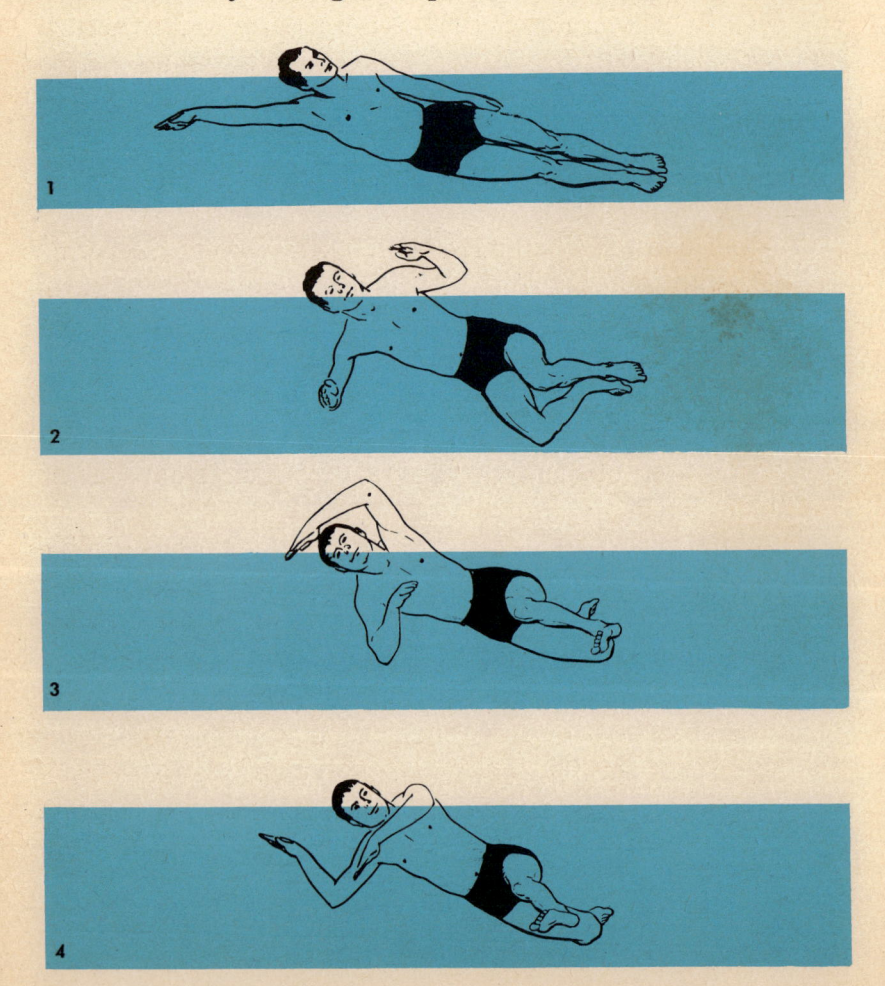

From the extended position on the thigh, the top arm is recovered out of water and is placed in the water slightly forward of the face, hand leading and ready for the propulsive phase of the arm action.

The action of the lower arm, the leg kicks, breathing, and coordination remain the same as described for the sidestroke in chapter 5.

Trudgen Strokes

With the de-emphasis of the kick in the crawl stroke and the recognition that some roll on the long axis of the body is necessary for effective stroking, many skilled swimmers and competitive swimmers are using variations of the crawl stroke that are quite similar to the trudgen.

Arm action and breathing in the trudgen are the same as described for the crawl stroke in chapter 5.

To perform the trudgen stroke, the swimmer performs a shortened scissors kick or even a more pronounced widening of the crawl kick as he rolls to breathe and press backward with the propelling arm. A swimmer who rotates his head to the left would time the positive action of the kick as his right arm is recovered forward. Following this leg action, the legs would trail for the remainder of the stroke cycle.

The trudgen crawl is another variation that is simple to perform. At the conclusion of the short scissors kick or widened crawl beat, and when the swimmer has returned to the prone position, he adds either two or four crawl kicks instead of allowing the legs to trail.

In the description of the crawl, it was emphasized that the leg action serves to balance and stabilize the effects of the roll and the arm swing. It can readily be understood that many swimmers naturally coordinate into some variation of the trudgen technique.

A coordinated trudgen stroke or variant is useful in swimming practically any distance or for approaching with good speed to a victim. With minor adjustment of the head position, good visibility in the lifesaving approach is also possible.

Inverted Breaststroke

The inverted breaststroke can be an effective and relaxed style of swimming on the back, especially for swimmers who possess good body buoyancy. As the name implies, it has some similarities to the breaststroke since it is an alternate, paired arm and leg action followed by a glide.

The starting and gliding position calls for a streamlined horizontal position, with back flat. Arms are fully extended in front of the head, with hands together and palms up and slightly under the surface. Legs are also extended, with the hips and feet just below the surface. The head is submerged to about the level of the ears, thus leaving the face out of water for free breathing.

From the extended position, the hands are pressed backwards all the way to the side for the positive action. The recovery must be accomplished gently and easily underwater to preserve the body balance and position. The hands are drawn along the sides to a position below the arm pits, at which point the fingers lead, palms turned up, and the hands are slid behind the ears to the fully extended gliding position.

The leg action is the inverted breaststroke kick as performed in the elementary backstroke, which is described in chapter 5.

The recommended coordination follows a press (arm action), kick (leg action), and glide. The arms will be pressed back almost to the sides before the legs start to recover. The positive leg action is executed as the arms are being extended behind the head. A moderate glide follows but should not be prolonged to a point where forward momentum is lost.

Butterfly Stroke

In its present form, the butterfly stroke is the newest of the competitive strokes. It does not have any direct application to lifesaving or to recreational swimming since in order to swim this stroke efficiently for any distance, conditioning and training is essential. As a recognized modern style of swimming, however, it presents a challenge for skilled swimmers to add to their watermanship by being able to perform this stroke.

BODY POSITION

The body is prone, arms and legs extended, head positioned with the waterline approximately at eye level, body flat and as streamlined as possible.

ARM ACTION

Basic mechanics of the arm action is similar to that of the arm action in the crawl stroke. Since the butterfly stroke is a paired movement and must be performed entirely in a prone position (*no* rolling to help propulsive action and recovery), certain modifications are essential. The hands enter the water simultaneously and approximately in front of the corresponding shoulders, palms facing downward. The hands slide laterally to the catch position, and then without pause the wrists and elbows are flexed as the pull starts backward along the shoulder line to the vertical. The push follows immediately to the full extension of the arms under the body.

Just prior to the elbows' becoming fully extended, the wrists are relaxed and the hands follow through into the rounding-off action. This follow-through momentum enables the arms to swing free and clear of the water for the recovery.

As the hands and arms clear the water in the recovery, the arms move outward and somewhat upward in a lateral movement. From the initial recovery position, the arms rotate medially to face the palms downward for the entry. The hands enter first, with the elbows slightly higher.

Butterfly Stroke

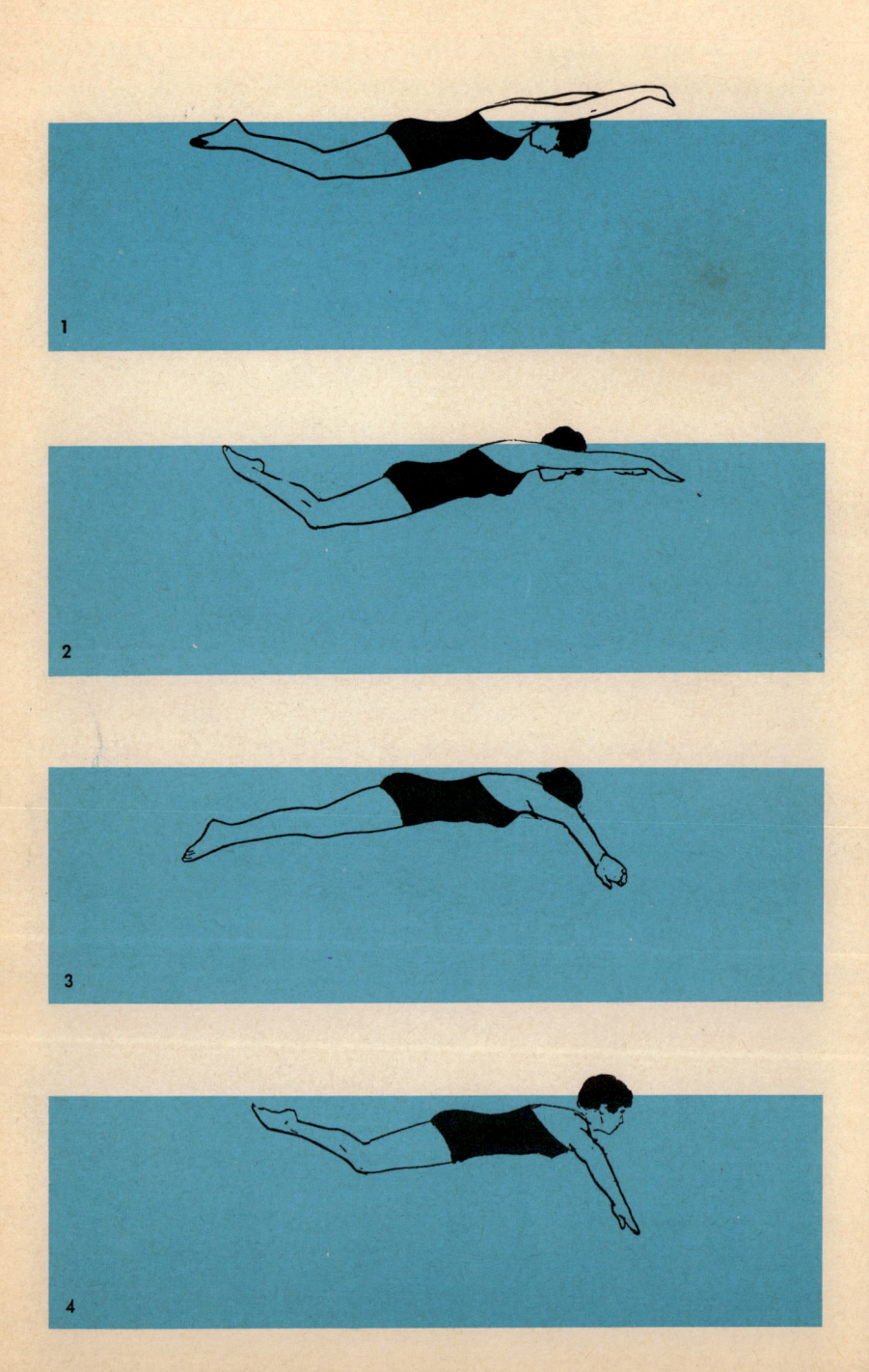

5

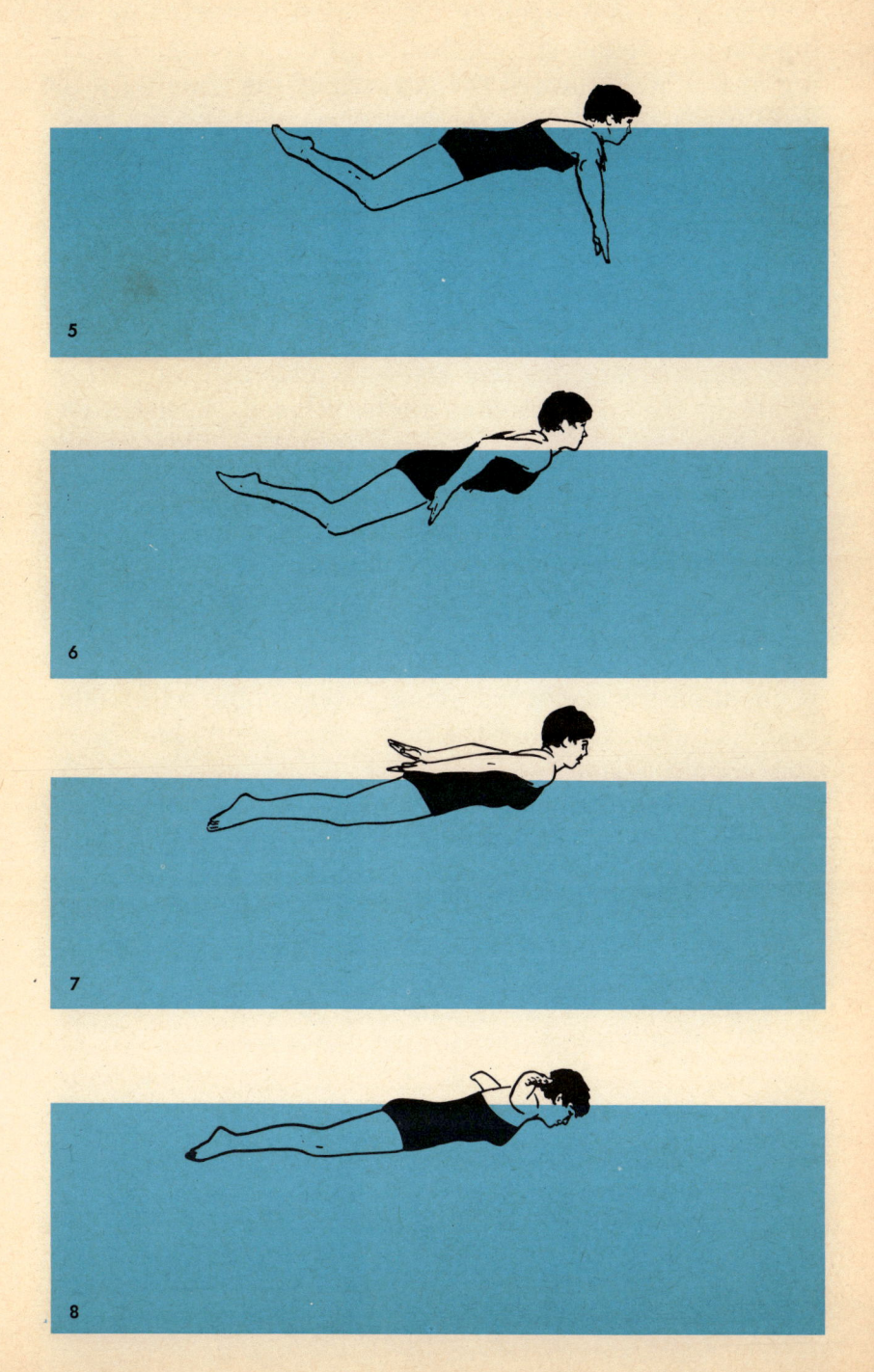

6

7

8

LEG ACTION

The leg action is the dolphin kick, which is performed in the same manner as the crawl kick with the exception that both legs act together. The action is started by lifting the hips followed by a flexion of the knees and a lifting of the heels toward the surface of the water. As the heels reach the surface, the hips start to drop, the knees continue to flex, and the toes are fully pointed. Maximum propulsion is obtained by simultaneously thrusting downward with both legs until the knees reach the hyperextended position, allowing the ankles and feet to follow through. The recovery begins again with the initial hip lift.

In the recovery, the feet are drawn toward the surface by flexing the knees, keeping ankles relaxed. When the feet have been drawn close to the surface, the ankles should move into a position of being extremely plantar-flexed. At the top of the recovery, the knees will be a little apart and the hips will have also flexed slightly. The legs are now in a position for the action. This is performed by a vigorous and sudden extension of the legs backward and somewhat downward. Since forward progress is dependent on the backward action, overkicking will simply result in overextending the downward action and therefore should be avoided.

Good ankle flexibility, in addition to strength in the hip muscles, knees, lower back, and abdominal wall, is necessary for an effective dolphin leg action.

BREATHING

The swimmer inhales through the mouth when it clears the water as the head is lifted by jutting the chin forward. Inhalation starts during the final phase of the backward push and ends when the arms leave the water at the start of the recovery. The head is then lowered as the arms are swung forward, and exhalation takes place through the mouth and nose during the completion of the arm cycle while the face is underwater. Some swimmers may prefer inhaling by a slight rotation of the head similar to the action in the crawl stroke.

COORDINATION

The recommended coordination is two kicks for each complete arm cycle. The first kick coincides with the hands moving through the first part of their propulsive action, while the second kick comes at the final phase of the push, the first being a major and the second being a minor kick. However, this difference in the positive action can be a natural development of the stroke since the first kick, which coincides with the initial positive arm action, will usually provide greater force.

RELATED AQUATIC SKILLS

Surface Diving

Surface diving is in reality a swimming skill. The ability to surface dive from a swimming position on the surface of the water to moderate underwater depths is a skill that is often used to rescue submerged victims and for personal enjoyment by those engaged in underwater activities. Surface dives can be performed in different ways and are classified as a pike surface dive, a tuck surface dive, a quick surface dive and a feetfirst or feetforemost surface dive.

Water depth for surface diving, in the early stages of the learner's development, should not exceed 6-8 feet. As skill and physical adjustment to water pressure improve, slightly deeper dives can be attempted. It must be remembered that pressure increases rather rapidly as a swimmer descends in the water. A broad guide of 1 pound per square inch for each 2 feet of descent emphasizes the pressure increase as one dives deeper. Since man lives under a normal atmospheric pressure of 14.7 pounds per square inch, a dive to a depth of 15 to 16 feet would result in a pressure of approximately 22 pounds. This amount of pressure sometimes causes pain in the ears, which can usually be alleviated by pinching the nose, closing the mouth, and forcing air through the eustachian tubes leading from the mouth to the ears.

Those suffering from ear or nose problems should consult their family physicians for advice concerning their participation in surface diving and underwater swimming activities.

PIKE SURFACE DIVE

As the name implies, this skill is performed with the legs in an extended position throughout the dive. Prior to initiating the dive, the swimmer should come to a position of full extension on the surface. Then, while still possessing momentum, he takes a breath of air and presses the arms back in a broad, sweeping, continuous motion toward the thighs. The beginning arm action is similar to the breaststroke movement but does not stop at the shoulders. This arm action, combined with a flexing at the hips, will bring the head underwater almost directly under the hips. At this point and without pause, the arms are circled forward vigorously, bringing the palms into a streamlined diving position, facing downward and together. The lifting of the extended legs occurs as part of both the reaction to this forward press of the arms and the extension of the hips. The body is now in a fully extended and streamlined position directed toward the bottom at a slight angle from the vertical. If these actions have been performed properly, the weight of the legs in this altered position should result in driving the body to a depth of about 8 feet without additional stroking of the arms and legs.

Exhaling gently through the nose during the dive will result in maintaining positive pressure and prevent water from entering the nasal passages.

TUCK SURFACE DIVE

The tuck surface dive is performed in the same manner as the pike with the exception of the leg action. During the forward action of the arms, the legs are drawn into a tuck position that results in reducing the length and weight movement of the leg area, thereby facilitating rotation into the head downward position. After the head and arms are streamlined and directed toward the bottom, the sudden extension of the legs will result in the descent.

Pike Surface Dive

QUICK SURFACE DIVE

The quick surface dive is a method of diving below the surface of the water from a swimming position when speed is necessary, such as in a situation in which a drowning victim disappears just before the rescuer reaches him. In this dive, the swimmer must have good forward momentum. To execute the dive, the swimmer takes a breath and extends the lead arm downward, and the other arm is recovered forward and downward to meet the extended arm. Without pause, the body is bent sharply at the hips, and the arms are pressed backward as the head starts downward. The sudden resistance of the water to the back of the body caused by the hip flexion and forward momentum enables the legs to be raised over the hips very easily without circling the arms forward as in the pike and tuck dives.

FEETFIRST SURFACE DIVE

The feetfirst or feetforemost dive is a method of diving deeply into murky water of unknown depth or bottom condition. Since the initial part of the dive involves a feetfirst descent, it is essential to raise the body sufficiently above the surface to provide the necessary weight to start its downward plunge. To do this, the swimmer first assumes the vertical position for treading water.

The swimmer then presses downward, with the hands going all the way to the sides, while executing a vigorous breaststroke or scissors kick. When the upper part of the body has risen to its highest point out of water, the body is streamlined by having the arms at the side, the legs extended, and the toes pointed. When the head sinks below the surface, the wrists are rotated to turn the palms upward and outward, and the swimmer presses vigorously upward, thus preserving the downward momentum.

As in the other surface dives, gently exhaling throughout the descent is advisable. This action often plunges the swimmer to a depth of at least 10 feet. Depending on the reason for the dive and the condition of the water and the bottom, the swimmer may elect to level off after his initial feetfirst downward plunge ceases or he can perform a tuck surface dive and swim to greater depths.

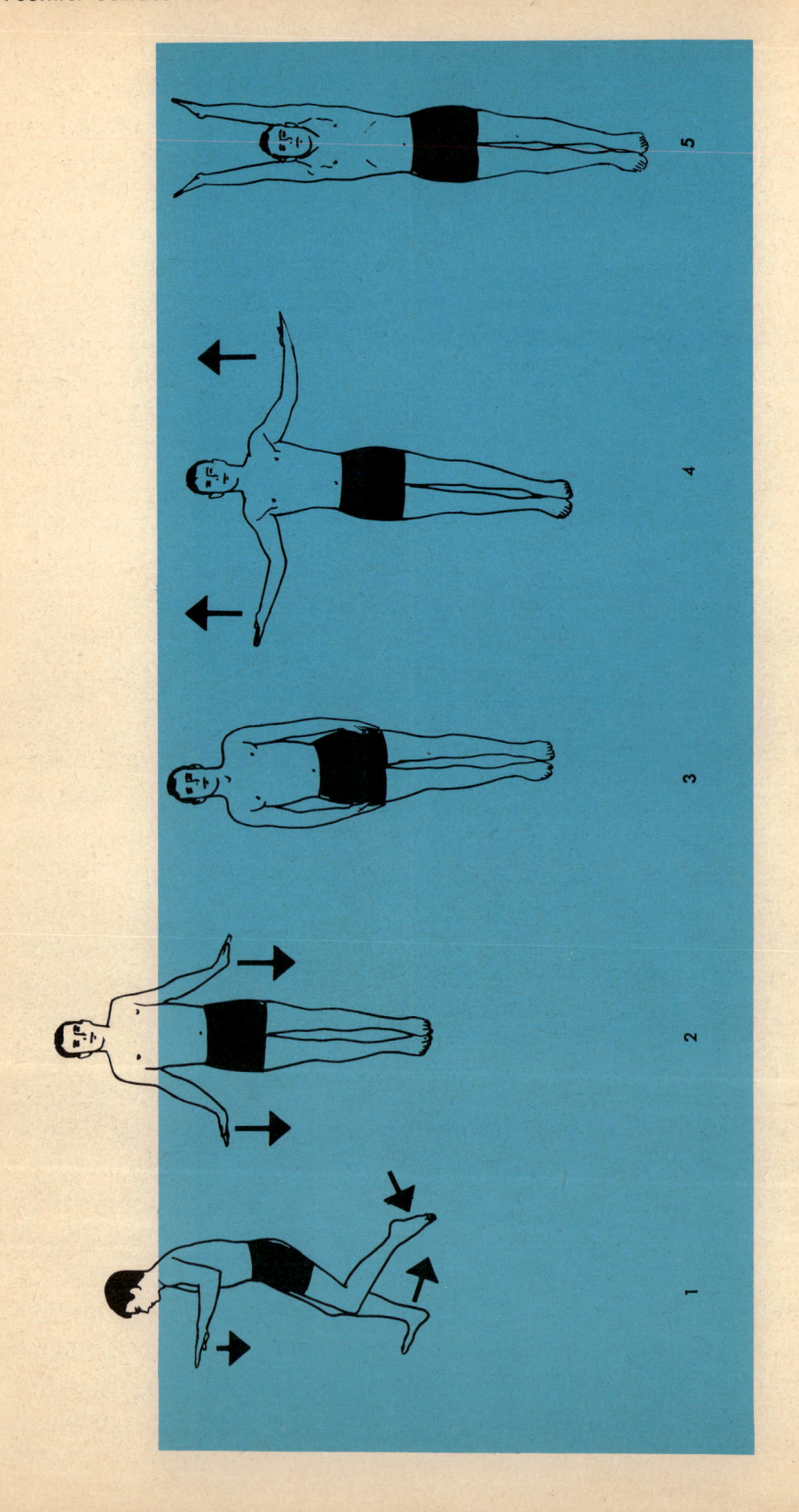

Feetfirst Surface Dive

Sculling

Sculling is a method of using the hands and arms to propel or support a swimmer in the water. When skillfully applied, it can be used effectively to maintain or change body positions in the water or to propel the swimmer in a desired direction and is especially useful in lifesaving and synchronized or stunt swimming. Expert watermanship and sculling are synonymous.

When the purpose of sculling is propulsion, the key to effective performance is to keep the wrists and elbows relaxed and the fingertips angled slightly upward toward the surface. For example, to scull on the back in the direction of the head, the arms start at the sides in an extended and relaxed position. From this starting position, the hands are first pressed outward, wrists leading, with the little fingers angled slightly toward the surface. The hands are then returned toward the body, wrists leading, with the thumbs now inclined slightly upward. This action should be continuous and fluid. The hands perform this skill with the elbows slightly flexed and the hands kept fairly close to the body. However, the distance that the hands move outward and back will vary according to the use being made of the sculling action.

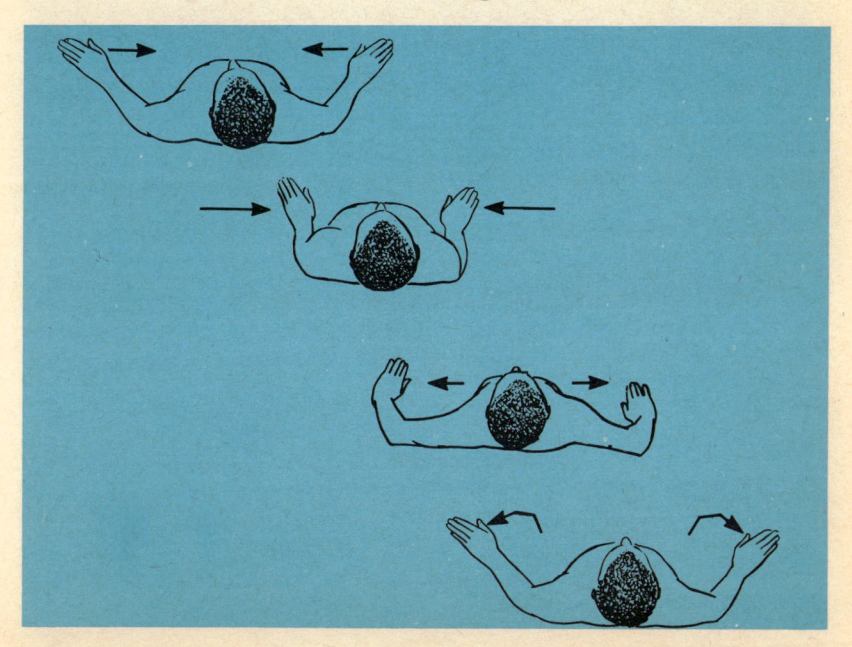

Treading Water

Treading water is a skill designed to support the head high enough out of the water to facilitate free breathing while keeping the body approximately in a vertical position. It is useful for lifesaving purposes, watching another swimmer, removing clothing, relief of cramps, and handling equipment.

Treading water is generally accomplished by using a single scissors action of the legs in conjunction with broad sculling movements of the hands and arms. These movements maintain the swimmer in an upright position with the head out of water. The arm action is started with arms apart in front of the swimmer, with elbows in a slightly bent position. The broad sculling movement of the arms and hands is a continuous underwater movement from the starting position in front of the body to an approximate line slightly forward of the shoulders, with the palms pressing almost directly downward throughout.

The single scissors kick employed is the standard sidestroke kick performed in a vertical position. The kick should be modified, however, so that it is slightly wider, and the kick finishes with the downward thrust and the legs not coming together, thus keeping a wider base of support. Such modification will tend to eliminate up-and-down or bobbing action.

The breaststroke kick is also effectively used by those having a strong breaststroke kick. Occasionally an individual with good knee flexibility and fine coordination will employ the "egg beater" kick. This is essentially a continuous, rhythmical, alternating action of the breaststroke kick.

Underwater Swimming

The skill of underwater swimming enables swimmers to recover lost objects, avoid surface hazards, and enjoy underwater activities. Many drownings have been prevented through the ability of rescuers to surface dive and search the bottom by swimming underwater.

SAFETY FACTORS

Swimmers with average skill rarely swim at depths greater than 10-15 feet and should not go deeper except to perform an emergency rescue or, after long practice, to engage in skin diving or other underwater activities. Distance underwater swimming should be discouraged, and the dangers of hyperventilating the lungs before swimming underwater should be thoroughly understood. Hyperventilation, or deep breathing, increases breath-holding time by blowing off carbon dioxide and thus lowering the amount of carbon dioxide in the blood. If, following hyperventilation, the swimmer attempts to swim underwater for distance, a considerable length of time may elapse before the carbon dioxide level, reduced by overbreathing, will provide a strong stimulus to breathe. The danger is that the the oxygen level may drop to a point where the swimmer "blacks out" before the carbon dioxide level increases to the point where the swimmer feels the urge to take a breath. Unless help is at hand to get him to the surface, drowning will result. All swimmers engaged in underwater swimming should be paired with a buddy and be closely supervised.

UNDERWATER STROKE

A modification of the breaststroke is generally the most efficient technique to use for underwater swimming. From a position of full extension, the breaststroke arm action is started. Instead of stopping the backward propulsive action in front of the shoulders, the swimmer continues to press the hands and arms directly backward. The action is completed as the elbows extend, palms facing backwards, until the arms are fully extended with the hands at the sides, palms up. This is the glide position in the underwater stroke.

Recovery of the arms is made by drawing the hands forward under and close to the body and finally to the fully extended position in front of the head. There is no glide in this position, and the arm propulsive action starts immediately.

The leg action is timed to finish in an extended position just as the arms are completing the backwards press and are at the sides for the glide position. The glide should be timed so that complete forward momentum is not lost before starting the recovery phase.

If the swimmer prefers, he may use a scissors kick in combination with the same full breaststroke arm action. When a scissors kick is used, the lower part of the body may be rotated slightly to enable the kick to be performed closer to a horizontal plane.

Direction and level can be changed by raising or lowering the head and by arm action of pressing upward at the end of the stroke or downward at the start of the arm movement. Flexing or extending at the hips will also result in some control in moving in a desired direction down or up. The swimmer should keep the eyes open in underwater swimming in order to see any possible obstructions.

When the swimmer is in dark or murky water or where underwater obstacles are present, the breaststroke arm action with modification should be used. This will give added protection by having the hands in front of the head most of the time since the arm action is virtually a short circular sculling action of the wrists with the arms extended.

Underwater Stroke

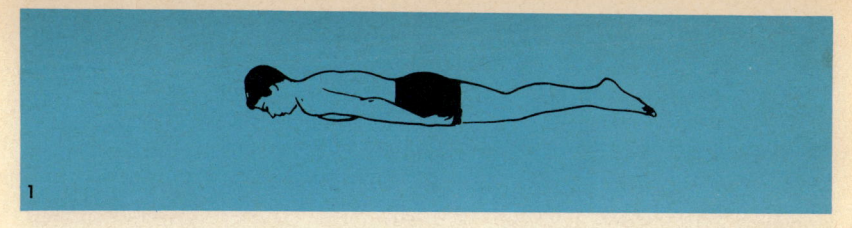

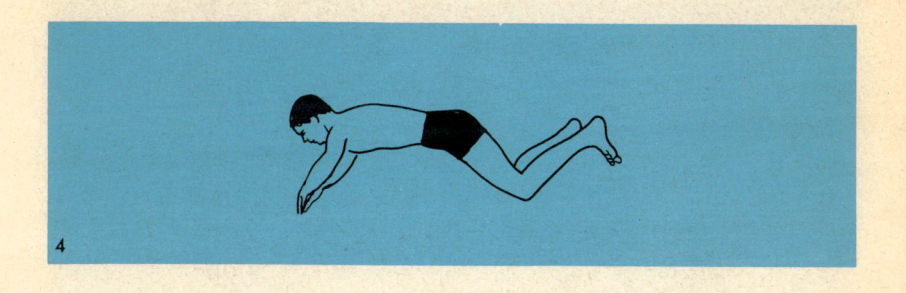

1

2

3

4

5

Other modification of strokes can be effectively used in underwater swimming. Where there is good visibility, a stroke on the side that employs a broad, sweeping backward action of both arms simultaneously may be used. In this stroke, the scissors kick is used and coincides with the arm action followed by a moderate glide. Another variation could be the breaststroke arm action combined with the crawl kick.

Front Start (Shallow Dive)

Commonly referred to as a racing start or dive, the front start is a long, low-projecting dive performed with a straight, streamlined body position that enables the swimmer to enter the water at a controlled angle of entry resulting in great forward momentum. Although used mostly in competitive events, the front start is useful for lifesaving in situations where speed is urgent and the entry can be made in water of known depth and free of underwater hazards.

The swimmer assumes a position on the starting platform or at the edge of the pool with the feet about 6 inches apart, toes gripping the edge and heels down. The knees are bent slightly, while the hips are bent to a point where the back is about parallel to the deck. The arms are extended loosely down and slightly back, the head is erect, and the eyes are focused on a spot well ahead of the swimmer.

The arms start the motion by a vigorous forward swing, circling slightly inward and then forward. This action will cause the body to move forward to a point where the spring or vigorous extension of the whole body will drive the body forward away from the wall in a line of flight nearly parallel to the surface.

There are many variations in the arm action. However, a simple arm movement that can be coordinated with the rapid extension of the knees, hips, and ankles will usually be more successful.

Front Start (Shallow Dive)

During the flight, the head drops slightly to a position between the outstretched arms, which are angled slightly downward. The entry should be as shallow as possible and still allow the diver to enter at a slight angle as opposed to hitting too large a surface of the body on the water and thereby retarding forward movement. The fully extended and streamlined position is maintained during the glide underwater until the swimmer feels some loss of momentum, at which time the first propulsive leg action will cause him to regain the surface and start stroking.

Starting on the Back

If no hand grips as found on regulation starting blocks are available, the hands grasp the edge of the pool or the trough approximately in front of the shoulders. The feet are firmly placed against the wall and slightly below the surface, while the body is in a crouched knee-to-chest position. In this start, the swimmer is attempting to coordinate his arm, head, and leg action to project his body out over the surface and to enter the water at a slight angle in order to best utilize the momentum thus derived for a maximum glide through the water.

The start is initiated by driving the arms sideways and backwards vigorously to a full arm extension position above the head. The head also drives backward simultaneously with the arms. A vigorous extension of the knees and hips follows with a final push or extension of the ankles to give added speed and push. This action propels the swimmer out over the surface, body stretched and slightly arched.

The hands enter first, and the head and body follow at a slight angle to present the least possible resistance. The depth of the glide is controlled by the hand and head movements. The glide should be continued until the swimmer feels that the momentum has lessened to about his swimming speed, at which time the leg action begins and is followed by the action of the arms. Exhalation through the nose throughout the underwater phase of the start is recommended to keep water out of the nasal passages.

Back Crawl Start

Turns

The majority of swimming instruction and practice today occurs in swimming pools. Since pools are somewhat confined areas for continuing practice, some ability in turning at the pool ends easily is important if such facilities are to be used effectively. Also, since many intermediate swimmers may participate in formal or informal competition, the ability to execute an effective turn involving strokes on the front and back is desirable. The turns described provide a simple treatment of these skills.

CRAWL STROKE TURN

As the swimmer approaches the wall or turning surface, the touch or contact is made with the hand of the extended arm. The elbow flexes to bring the head close to the wall, and the body rolls on the side of the extended arm. The free arm hooks the water back to facilitate bringing the body into a compact tuck position and to help rotate the body in the direction of the free arm. The final rotation is made with the feet in contact with the wall, and the compactly tucked body stays close to the turning surface.

The head initiates the change of body direction while the forward arm extends and pushes away from the wall. Inhalation occurs as the face clears the surface. The forward arm is then placed alongside the free arm, and at this stage both arms will be flexed but pointed in the line of travel away from the wall.

The head is now submerged between the arms, and the body is under the surface and momentarily poised for the pushoff phase.

From the compact crouched position, the arms extend fully as the swimmer pushes off vigorously. The rapid extension of the body results in a streamlined glide position that angles slightly upward to the surface. The glide position is held until the swimmer's hands reach the surface and the momentum from the pushoff starts to lessen. Exhalation through the nose should start with the push from the wall.

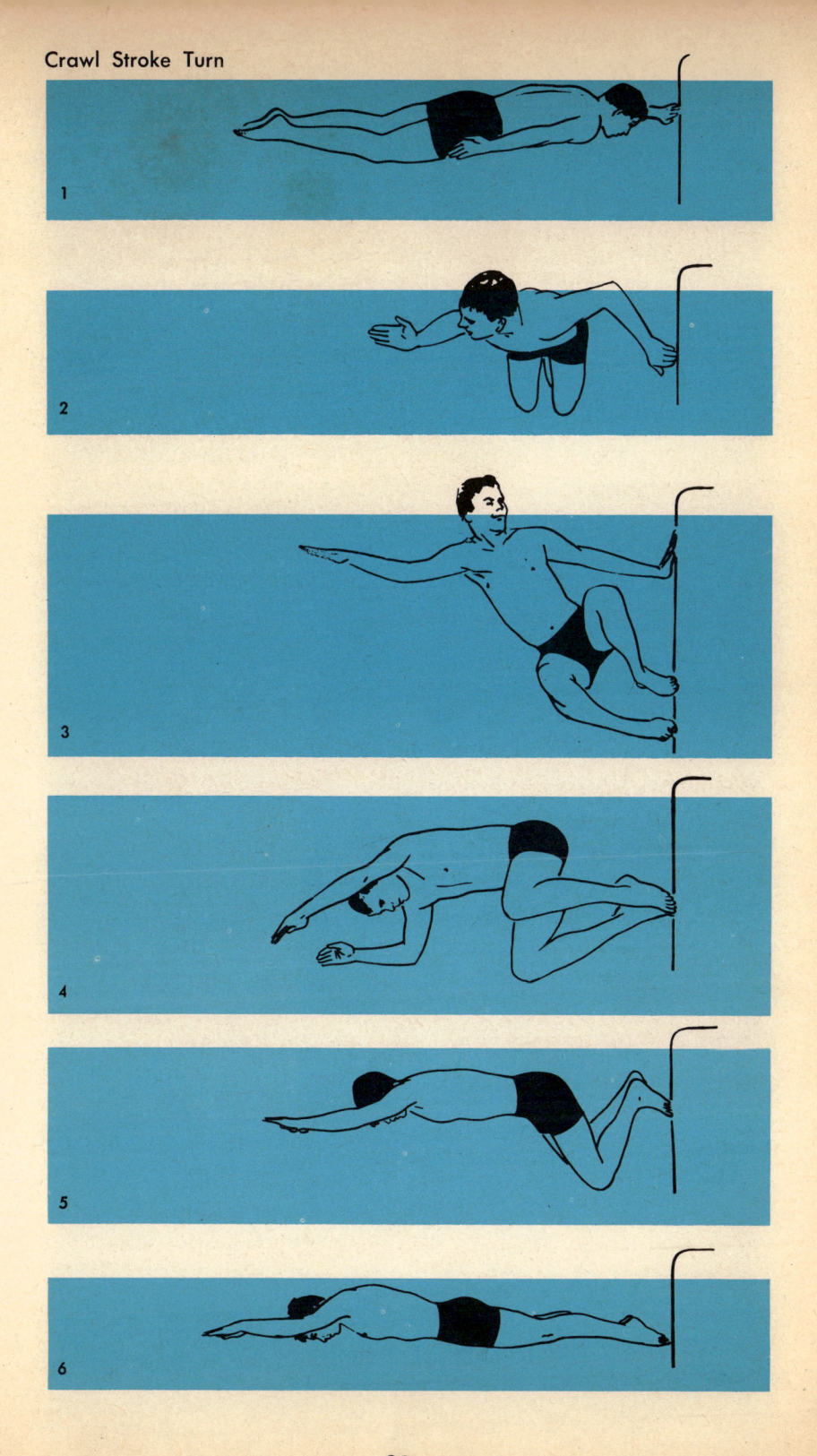

Crawl Stroke Turn

BREASTSTROKE AND BUTTERFLY TURN

Since this turn should be made with both hands touching the turning surface at the same time and on an even plane, some modification of the crawl stroke turn will be necessary.

The swimmer comes to the wall with both arms extended and makes contact with both hands simultaneously and still at the same level. The elbows flex, bringing the head close to the wall as the body is tucked up into a compact position.

The head initiates the rotation of the body in the desired direction. For example, if the swimmer desires to turn to the right, the head will turn to the right to initiate rotation in that direction. The arms extend by pushing away from the wall and thus give impetus to the change of direction.

Inhalation occurs as the head is turned and the body is changing direction. As the head turns, the hand on the turning side will move from contact with the wall to a position in front of the head. As the body continues to rotate, the other hand leaves the wall, is drawn through the water, and comes alongside the other hand, elbows still flexed, palms down.

The swimmer should now be in a crouched and compact position, head submerged between the arms and body poised for the pushoff similar to the position described for the crawl turn.

SIDESTROKE TURN

For swimmers who wish to continue practicing a sidestroke, the crawl stroke turn can be used with some variation. Contact with the wall can be made with the lead arm, and the entire turn can be executed as described for the crawl stroke turn. While the body still has sufficient momentum during the glide after the pushoff, the swimmer can simply rotate the body to the desired side for continued practice.

BACKSTROKE TURN

To execute a turn to the right, the swimmer would gauge his approach to the turning surface and contact the wall with the right hand, palm flat against the surface and thumb up. The swimmer rolls on the right as the elbow flexes to bring the swimmer closer to the wall.

The knees are drawn up close to the chest into a tuck position, and the body spins to the right toward the wall. The left arm pushes back and away against the water to facilitate the spinning action. The spin continues until the swimmer's feet are against the wall below the surface, and the body is now in a knee-to-chest crouched position with both hands against the wall in front of the shoulders. NOTE. When a swimmer has mastered these steps, the left arm need not be brought to the wall. Instead, as soon as it has pushed back and away and the spin is completed, this arm can initiate the action of the head and shoulders being placed in the water as described below.

At this point, the swimmer inhales, lets his hips settle lower in the water, and rocks his head and shoulders gently back into the water. Still staying close to the wall, the hands are gently drawn to the shoulders, in which position the palms are turned up, and, with fingers leading, the hands are then extended above the head but still submerged.

The swimmer now pushes off from the wall as the arms fully extend, and the body in a fully streamlined position angles gradually to the surface.

Exhalation should begin through the nose as soon as the head lies back and should continue until the face breaks water at the completion of the glide.

Turns should be practiced on both sides so that the swimmer can then turn effectively on the lead arm that contacts the turning surface.

Backstroke Turn

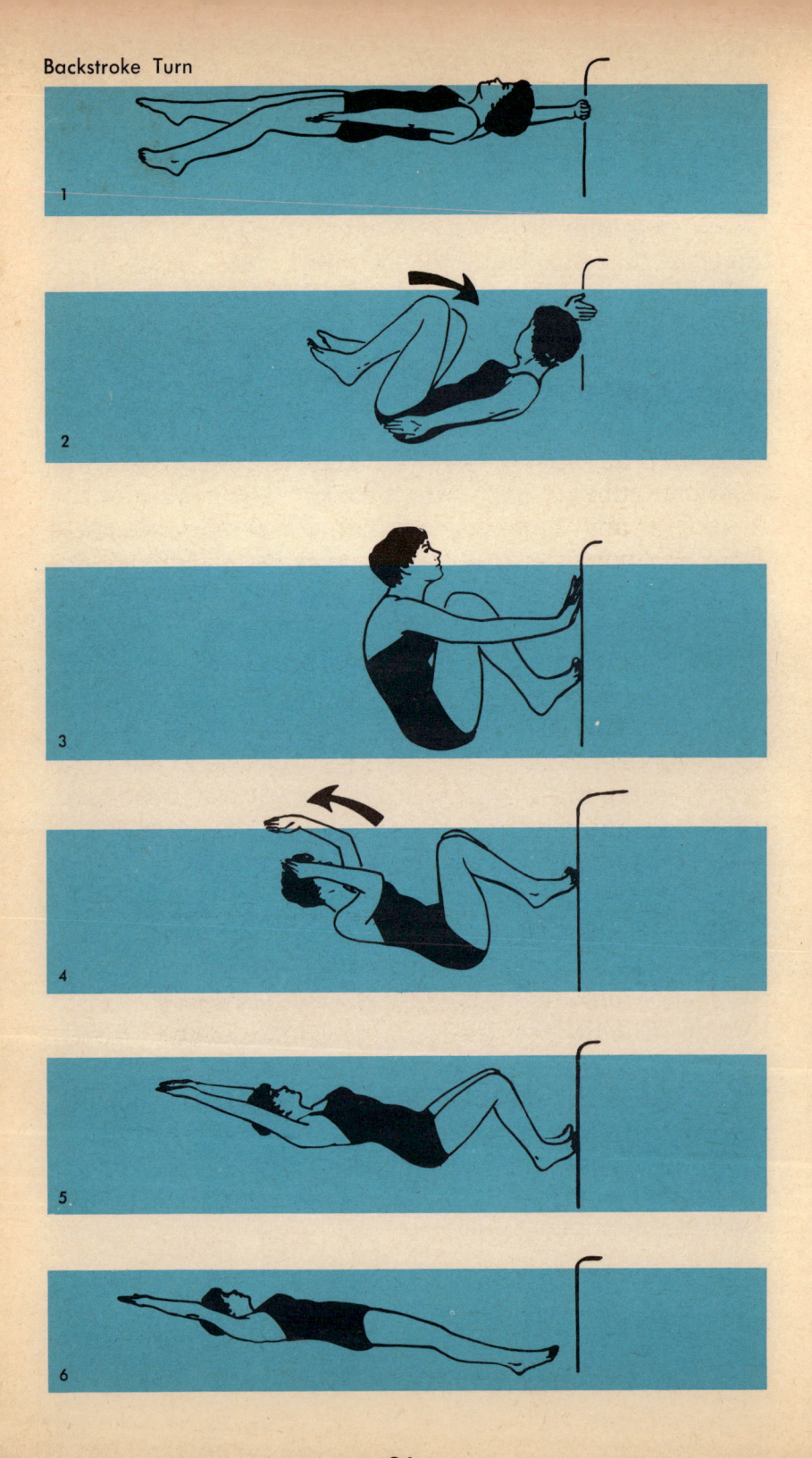

8

DIVING

The word "dive" is often used to describe different ways of entering and descending beneath the surface of the water. While most people associate the term with a headfirst entry, it is also applied to designate a feetfirst entry, such as a somersault dive from a springboard. To a skin or scuba diver the word "dive" might mean surface diving and swimming down to a desired depth. The diving information presented in this chapter is concerned with diving fundamentals, safety, headfirst entries, progressive steps relating to learning how to dive, and the performance of a coordinated standing and running front dive from a deck and springboard.

Additional information on competitive diving, including rules, degree of difficulty tables, listing of dives in the five categories, recommended standard dimensions for diving equipment and facilities, and judging, can be found in the current editions of the following publications:

Official Handbook: Swimming, Diving, Water Polo (published by the Amateur Athletic Union)
Official Collegiate and Scholastic Swimming Guide (published by the National Collegiate Athletic Association)
Aquatics Guide (published by the Division for Girls and Women's Sports, American Association for Health, Physical Education and Recreation)

Diving Fundamentals

Most swimmers like to dive, but very few become highly skilled in the art of diving. Body structure, balance, courage, motivation, perseverence, and kinesthetic sense, as well as good coaching, all contribute to the development of a skilled performer. Of these attributes, kinesthetic awareness rates high in determining whether an individual is likely to become a skilled diver. Kinesthetic awareness may be described as the ability of an individual to be aware of his position in space at any time and of the relationship of all parts of his body to each other and to his center of movement. As an example, a skilled diver, when performing an intricate dive, can control his spinning and twisting movements and coordinate his arms and legs to execute the dive while in the air and still maintain necessary control to complete the dive with a good entry into the water. Since this is an endowed characteristic, it may help to understand why some individuals with poor kinesthetic sense experience problems when learning to dive. Kinesthetic awareness can be improved in an individual through diving practice in which constant emphasis is on keeping the eyes open and focused on specific points or objects during the performance of the dive.

Diving calls for an understanding of the importance of the weight of the head as it moves around a pivotal point. Most beginners have experienced dropping the head too quickly in a dive, resulting in an "overthrow" and causing the diver to land flat on his back. Such an experience painfully teaches the lesson of head control and its importance to a dive.

Another factor that contributes to the development of a skilled diver is muscle control when executing a dive and making the entry. The control of abdominal, back, and leg muscles will be necessary in order to enter the water with the proper extension and alignment of the body joints. Many novices fail to exercise proper control or tensing of these muscles when diving and, as a result, enter the water in various stages of collapse. Such entries may cause neck, shoulder, and back strains, particularly if the dive is made from a springboard or heights. It should also be remembered that if an individual is cold from repeated dives into cold water and exposure to cool air, his physical and mental ability to execute the dive properly is impaired and may be a cause of injury.

When the diver enters the water in a headfirst dive, the arms are extended beyond the head in the line of flight, with hands together and palms down, to help relieve the impact of the water on the top of the head and to avoid injury by contact with the bottom if the dive is deeper than expected. As previously indicated, unless the learner is cautioned to tense his arm and shoulder muscles, his arms may be forcefully flung aside because of the resistance of the water as he enters, causing painful injury.

Feetfirst entries are made with the legs pressed close together and arms pressed tightly to the sides. Upon entry, the diver exhales forcefully through the nose to prevent water from entering the nasal passages.

Diving Safety

Of primary importance to diving safety is having ample water depth for the height of the dive and the individual. Competitive standards call for a minimum depth of 10 feet for a 1-meter board. For outdoor diving areas, the bottom should be cleared of stumps, rocks, and other obstacles. Diving boards should be mounted on a firm foundation and never on an insecure base, such as a float that can be affected by shifting weight loads and wave action.

Regulation diving boards are 16 feet long by 20 inches wide, with the entire length of the top surface adequately covered with nonskid material. The standard height of the board above water is 1 meter (39.37 inches), although for small children it can be lowered to 20-24 inches. For safety, the front end of the board should project at least 6 feet beyond the end of the pool or dock. Clearance from the sides of the board should be at least 10 feet, and the distance between diving boards should be at least 8 feet. If additional boards are planned, they should not be more than 1 meter in height unless expert diving instruction and supervision is available and board use is restricted to skilled divers. Many diving injuries have been caused by poor divers diving from a poorly supervised 3-meter board. A diving board should be installed so that it is level, as a pitched board tends to cause the diver to come back down on the board when he dives. To sum up, diving boards should be located so that the execution and entry of the dive are not interfered with by the pool sides, the slant of the pool bottom, overhead structures, and other diving structures even if the diver "misses" a dive resulting in out-of-line flight and entry.

Manufacturers develop diving boards of fiberglass, laminated materials, and aluminum. The selection of the board will depend on its use and the average age level of the group participating. A good board, properly mounted, with an adjustable fulcrum, is a worthwhile investment for safety and will stimulate diving interest.

Rules and regulations concerning board use and diving restrictions should be posted and understood. One of the most important of these rules is: *Never start a dive until the preceding diver has come to the surface and moved from the diving entry area.* Compliance with this rule will be much easier if ladders are strategically located to force the diver to swim to a side removed from the diving entry area when getting out of the pool after his dive.

Faulty diving technique sometimes causes a diver to land flat. Such a landing is painful but not dangerous if the dive is executed from a low board or elevation. Skilled divers learn to protect themselves by "balling up" just before they hit the water after a "missed" dive.

An individual having a history of nasal, ear, or sinus problems should consult his family physician before participating in diving programs.

Progression for the Beginner

When a beginner has learned to swim well enough to be comfortable and safe in deep water, he is ready to learn how to dive into deep water. Prior to actual diving, however, skills such as porpoise diving, performing handstands in standing-depth water, recovering from a feet-first entry in deep water, and bobbing will build confidence and make the initial step much easier.

The basic progression is designed to give the learner a gradual adjustment starting from a position close to the water and graduating to a dive from a standing position. It may have to be varied, however, depending on the facility. For instance, where there is no overflow trough or brace for the feet, it might be necessary and advisable to start from the one-knee position. Progress may be uneven. It sometimes may be necessary to go back for more practice to a previous step when the learner experiences difficulty at a particular level.

Even at the beginning stage, however, there are some fundamentals that must be understood since habits formed at the beginning stage could affect a person's diving ability and enjoyment for a lifetime. The major emphasis should be on keeping the eyes open and focused properly, position of arms and head, body control for a good entry, and, finally, surfacing.

The learner must be taught to keep the eyes open so that he can see and judge where he is at all times. Keeping the arms in line with the head will control the angle of entry. The body can be controlled for proper entry and subsequent glide by the learner's making a conscious effort to tense or contract abdominal and leg muscles to get full alignment and extension of body joints to prevent overthrow or collapse.

SITTING

Step 1—sit

Sitting on the edge or deck, with heels resting on the pool overflow trough, ladder rung, or suitable brace, the beginner extends the arms, pressing his biceps against the ears. The hands are together, thumbs pressing against each other, and the eyes should be open and focused on a spot about 3 feet away. A breath is taken, the upper body bends forward, and, when ready, the beginner rolls in. When entirely in the water, he can raise the head and arms and surface. Separating the legs and rolling in between his knees may help the learner to enter the water at the proper angle.

Repeated efforts will add confidence, allowing the learner to go deeper and hold the extended glide position. Many learners will have a tendency to lift the head before entering the water, to fail to straighten the legs, to roll over or somersault underwater, or to lift the head too soon underwater. Such faults should be corrected before progressing to the next step.

ON ONE KNEE

The progression leading to a standing position may be fairly rapid once the learner has adjusted to the head-foremost entry. In this step, the learner kneels on one knee and assumes the correct head and arm position. With eyes open and focused on the entry spot, he leans forward and rolls into the water. The same faults as mentioned for the previous step may be in evidence and should be corrected by further practice.

Step 2—one knee   Step 3—tip-in

STANDING

From a position at the edge, the first effort should be to assume the correct head and arm position and, when ready, simply to tip forward and glide. Practice should correct the faults of flipping over, keeping the knees bent, and raising the head too soon. Before the learner proceeds to the next step, his form should be reasonably good and well controlled.

Step 4—fall-in   Step 5—small spring

ADDING A LEG SPRING

The arm position remains the same as in the preceding step in order to simplify the learning process. The learner stands at the edge, body erect, and bends the knees slightly.

Standing dive with small spring (Step 5)

The spring is a rapid extension of the knees as the body starts to balance a little forward. The arm and head position is kept constant as the body stretches up and over, in an arc, and enters the water in a controlled head-first position.

COORDINATING LEG SPRING WITH ARM ACTION

Standing at the edge with toes gripping, arms forward, body erect, the learner brings the arms down as the knees bend, and the arm lift is coordinated with the spring or extension of the knees. This action is followed by a stretching up and over an imaginary line and down into the water with the arms pressing against the head and the hands together. The position is held until the whole body has submerged.

This simple coordination of arm and leg action is also basic to takeoffs from a springboard.

Takeoff push coordination

Standing Front Dive From Board

Since diving from a springboard usually brings on problems of added height and the action of the board itself, the first adjustment should be to the added height. From a position at the end of the board, the learner should practice a simple forward tip-in dive, with emphasis on the arm and head position, control of entry, and body position. Until this step can be performed with ease and confidence, any use of board action should be discouraged.

The next step is virtually to duplicate the timing used in the coordinated front dive from the deck. The addition is getting adjusted to the action of the board and the timing involved. The diver stands at the end of the board, body and head erect, arms extended in front of the body, and eyes focused on the entry point. As the knees bend, the arms come down, pressing the board down slightly, and then they come up and forward as the whole body extends and stretches in a fairly small arc toward the water. The most common fault is to lose body control and to flip over. The board impetus should be almost straight up and the arm and leg action timed to push the diver up instead of out. Practice on this step will teach added body control, build confidence, and give experience in the spring and actions of the board.

Running Front Dive From Board

A running front dive from a springboard can be divided into three basic phases: the approach, the execution of the dive in the air, and the entry.

The completed running front dive described should result in a smooth and effective approach, a flight through the air in a simple arc, and a good entry.

FORWARD APPROACH

The approach is really the boardwork or the necessary things that are performed on the board in order to achieve sufficient height to perform the flight in the air. Further defined, the approach should consist of at least three steps, the hurdle, and a takeoff from both feet at the end of the board.

The steps are really a rhythmic accelerated walk. The hurdle lifts the diver up, enabling him to return the upright body down on the board, thereby causing the board to bend. The action of the board as it comes upward helps to lift the diver into the air. The entire approach should be performed smoothly and naturally.

To approach properly, the diver must first estimate his starting position on the board. To do this, he stands about 1 foot from the end of the board and takes three normal steps and a hurdle toward the "inboard" end. This spot should be his approximate starting position, allowing him to then take three steps and a hurdle and land on both feet close to the end of the board.

Initially, the diver will start off with the foot that feels natural. In fact, the choice of feet may change as soon as the learner becomes aware of which foot is the best one to take off from into the hurdle. If this is the right foot, then the approach will start by stepping off with that foot, and vice versa.

The diver takes a position at his estimated starting line, feet together, body erect, arms at the side with fingers extended naturally, and eyes focused on the end of the board. The first step is a normal step, the second is slightly longer, and the third is again longer and more forceful. The arms during the first two steps can hang naturally at the side. During the third step, the arms are slightly behind the body in preparation for their forward and upward lift during the hurdle. As the diver comes down with his forward foot on his third step, the opposite knee bends and is brought up simultaneously with the raising of the arms. As the arms have reached the extended position over the head, the raised thigh should be at right angles to the body. The pushing leg extends strongly and stays extended until the landing. This coordinated action projects the diver up into the air and over the board.

Correct boardwork

As the diver starts to descend, the knee that is flexed should straighten out just before landing on the board. The body should be aligned so that the weight is over the extended leg, while the eyes are still focused on the board tip and the head is erect. Keeping the body vertical, the diver contacts the board with the balls of the feet, followed immediately by the entire sole of the foot, and then the knees flex and there is a slight flexion at the hips. At the same time, the arms descend quickly to the side as the weight resulting from the entire descent depresses the board.

Timing his actions with the start of the board's reacting upward, the diver coordinates the arm lift with a vigorous extension of the body, driving the diver upward. Constant practice under the watchful eye of a competent instructor will be helpful to perfect a smooth and effective approach, which is fundamental to good diving.

ENTRY

The body should enter the water a little short of being vertical since the body will continue to rotate as it enters the water. The diver actually aims for a particular spot and must maintain necessary muscular tension to keep the body in alignment. When a diver attempts to go into the water vertically, the body will continue to move in the direction of rotation, resulting in poor entry with the dive going over.

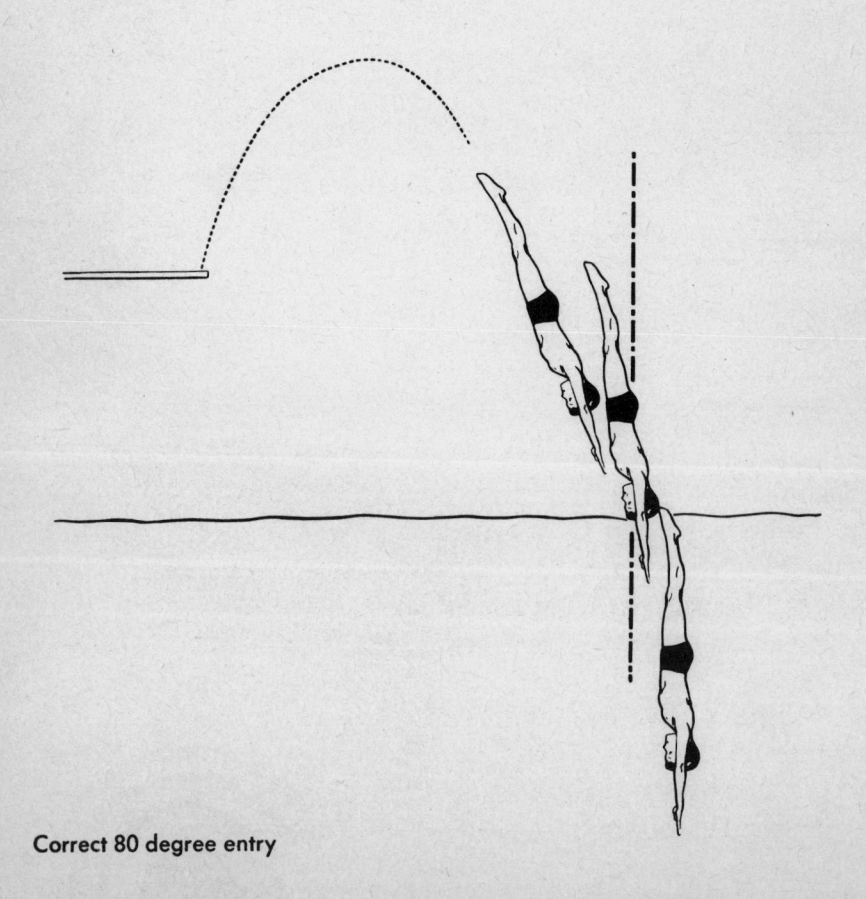

Correct 80 degree entry

BASIC RUNNING FORWARD DIVE

The forward dive that should be practiced and perfected is now one which results in the diver attaining a fair amount of height, going up and over an imaginary line, and the body following through in a simple arc. The diver enters the water at an angle that is a little less than vertical and continues down to the bottom, keeping his body in good control and alignment.

The learner should strive for an approach that results in a minimum of three steps that are done smoothly, leading into a hurdle that is coordinated with the upswing of the arms. A good descent and takeoff follow, with the arms stretching upward into the flight of the body through the air in a simple arc.

Good control and mastery of the basic running forward dive can now lead into the more advanced diving skills.

9

SAFETY IN AQUATICS

Drownings in the United States have averaged about 7,000 yearly during the past few years. This statistic would seem to imply that the concentrated efforts of the Red Cross and other agencies in the field of water safety have not been successful. However, the number of yearly drownings alone does not give an accurate picture.

Millions of Americans have learned to swim since Commodore Wilbert E. Longfellow launched his "Waterproof America" crusade in 1914. The founder of the American Red Cross Water Safety Program built his campaign on the slogan "Every American a swimmer, every swimmer a lifesaver." Before this nationwide effort began, the drowning rate was 10.2 per hundred thousand population. Today, as a result of the combined efforts by many agencies and organizations, the rate is approximately 3.6 per 100,000 population. When one considers the tremendous increase in population and participation, it is then evident that water safety instruction and education have proved to be a successful approach in reducing the number of fatalities. For example, if the drowning rate of 10.2 per 100,000 were in effect today, more than 20,000 drownings would have occurred in this country last year as opposed to the figure of about 7,000 drownings.

Drownings can occur any place where there is water. National Safety Council statistics of drownings around the home show that individuals have drowned in bathtubs, wells, cisterns, cesspools, and even casual water as well as in swimming pools. Only about 40 percent of the yearly drownings occur to people who are swimming or playing in the water. The remainder, or 60 percent, occur in the classification of nonswimming fatalities due to accidentally falling into the water from docks, decks of pools, bridges, or shores, recreational boating and fishing accidents, and accidents in the home or on home premises.

It is estimated that over 100 million individuals each year engage in some form of aquatic endeavor. No longer confined to the category of being a luxury, over 500,000 residential swimming pools are in existence today. The construction of water conservation facilities and dams, huge lakes, and reservoirs have created recreational aquatic facilities where none existed previously. The farm pond, which was originally intended for watering livestock, fire protection, and irrigation, has become today's version of the "ole swimmin' hole" in rural areas. There are now well over a million of these ponds, and the number grows steadily larger each year. Since many of these ponds are equipped with docks, floats, diving boards, and boats of varying types and are even stocked with fish, they provide an outlet for aquatic recreation. Keeping pace with the growth of facilities has been the increased availability and refinement of the equipment needed for such myriad outlets as skin and scuba diving, water skiing, recreational boating, fishing, and surfing.

The need for everyone to be able to swim well enough to survive is evident. Nonswimmers and novice swimmers account for the majority of drownings. The large number of drownings occurring to young children when left unguarded even for a few moments points to the need for more education for all adults and parents. Supervision at all times, especially when it concerns young children, is a must.

Since a majority of drownings occur because people violate or ignore good safety practices, an attempt will be made to categorize such recommended procedures under the following:

1. Personal water safety
2. Safety at home pools
3. Safety at farm ponds

4. Safety at beaches
5. Helping others in an emergency
6. Helping yourself in an emergency
7. Survival floating

Personal Water Safety

1. Learn to swim well enough to survive in an emergency.
2. Never swim alone and swim only with a buddy who has the ability to help when necessary.
3. Swim only in supervised areas.
4. Follow rules set up for the particular pool, beach, or waterfront where you are swimming.
5. Learn the simple and safe reaching rescues.
6. Know how to administer artificial resuscitation.
7. Know your limitations and do not overestimate your ability.
8. Stay out of the water when overheated and immediately after eating.
9. Stay out of the water during electrical storms.
10. Dive only into known waters of sufficient depth.
11. Do not substitute inflated tubes, air mattresses, or other artificial supports for swimming ability.
12. Always swim a safe distance away from diving boards and platforms.
13. Avoid long periods of immersion and overexposure to the sun.
14. Take instruction under qualified instructors before participating in such aquatic sports as skin and scuba diving and water skiing.
15. Call for help only when you really need it.

Safety at Home Pools

1. Never permit anyone to swim alone. Constant and responsible supervision is a must. No child should

be left unattended in the pool area even for the length of time it takes to answer a telephone.

2. Have adequate fencing and a gate with a lock to prevent children from unauthorized entry.

3. Keep basic rescue and lifesaving equipment always available.

4. Post emergency instructions and telephone numbers conspicuously.

5. Have an adequate first aid kit available.

6. Enforce commonsense safety rules at all times. At least one responsible person should know how to administer artificial respiration and give intelligent first aid.

7. Clearly mark the deep and shallow sections. Separate the deep and shallow water by use of a buoyed line whenever weak swimmers or nonswimmers are using the pool.

8. Do not allow running, pushing, or boisterous play on the deck.

9. Encourage responsible parents or other adults to give water safety and swimming instruction to youngsters. (A recommended text is the American Red Cross booklet *Teaching Johnny To Swim*.)

10. Make sure there is adequate filtration to maintain good clarity of the water. Consult the local health department for regulations on pool sanitation.

11. Do not permit bottles, glasses, and sharp objects in or around the pool area.

12. Observe applicable personal safety rules, such as not swimming immediately after eating or when overheated or during an electrical storm; use of inflated objects by nonswimmers; and diving only in known and safe depths.

- Home pool
- Residential man-made lake

RED CROSS SAFETY POST

- Iced-over pond
- Farm pond

A "safety post," which is shown above, will provide basic rescue and lifesaving equipment that can be invaluable in emergencies. Attached to the post are a long reaching pole and an inflated inner tube affixed to a length of line. This equipment can be used to assist a person in trouble by reaching or throwing. The post is capped with a can to which are affixed instructions on the elementary forms of rescue and a description of artificial respiration techniques. (This information, as well as step-by-step directions for making the safety post, is given on American Red Cross Poster 1021 and is available through local Red Cross chapters.)

Safety at Farm Ponds

1. Never swim alone.
2. Mark off safe swimming areas with buoyed lines. Remove underwater snags, trash, bottles, and the like.
3. Avoid swimming areas immediately in front of steep-sloping banks.
4. Post warning signs at danger points.
5. Supervise children at *all* times.
6. Have water checked and approved by the local health department and recheck it periodically if used for swimming.
7. If practical, erect an adequate fence and a gate with a lock to prevent unauthorized entry by children.
8. Keep basic rescue and lifesaving equipment always available.
9. Post emergency instructions and telephone numbers.
10. Have an adequate first aid kit available.
11. Enforce commonsense safety rules. At least one responsible person should know how to administer artificial respiration, perform basic reaching rescues, and give intelligent first aid.
12. Have a responsible adult start water safety and swimming instruction for potential farm pond users. (A recommended text is the American Red Cross booklet *Teaching Johnny To Swim*.)
13. Make sure that piers, rafts, and landings are well built and securely braced.
14. Observe applicable personal safety rules such as not swimming immediately after eating, when overheated, or during an electrical storm; use of inflated objects by nonswimmers; and diving only in known and safe depths.

15. If pond is used for skating, add a ladder to the safety post as helpful emergency equipment.
16. To avoid accidents on the ice: Never skate alone. Skate only on a safe thickness of ice. Maintain supervision at all times. Skate in a restricted area.

Safety at Beaches

1. Swim in areas supervised by a lifeguard.
2. Never swim alone.
3. Check with a lifeguard regarding beach and surf conditions before swimming.
4. Report any unsafe beach condition to the lifeguard.
5. If you are being pulled offshore by a rip current, do not panic and do not try to buck the current. Swim parallel to shore across the current and, once free, then swim to shore.
6. Call or wave for help if unable to swim out of a strong current.
7. Never fake trouble or calls for help.
8. Never substitute the use of floating devices for swimming ability.
9. Do not use breakable objects on the beach, and, if any are found, pick them up and dispose of them for your own protection and the safety of others.
10. Do not dive into unknown water or into shallow-breaking waves.
11. Do not overestimate your ability by attempting long-distance swims. Swimming parallel to shore is safer and just as much exercise.
12. Continue supervision of small children even where there are lifeguards.
13. Do not swim close to piers or pilings.
14. Avoid sand throwing or any kind of horseplay.
15. Do not engage in unnecessary conversation with a lifeguard.

16. Observe applicable personal safety rules, such as not swimming immediately after eating or when overheated or during an electrical storm.
17. Respect the judgment and experience of the trained lifeguards, follow their advice, and do not interfere with the performance of their duty.

Helping Others in an Emergency

Since many unnecessary drownings occur within a few feet of safety, it is often possible for the untrained swimmer or even the nonswimmer to effect a nonswimming rescue. Such individuals should avoid personal contact wherever possible and should always be certain to maintain firm contact with the shore. The rescuer's weight on the shore or the deck should be kept low or slanting backward, and if possible the rescuer should use some piece of equipment.

The recommended procedure for effecting a nonswimming rescue is as follows.

1. If the victim is within arm reach:

Lie flat on deck of pool or dock and extend one arm toward victim. Take a firm grasp of deck or dock with the other arm, grab victim's wrist or arm, and draw the victim slowly to safety.

2. If the victim is beyond arm reach:
   Extend arm reach by using such items as shirt, towel, coat, branch, or pole. Allow the victim to grasp one end of the extended article and then pull him slowly to safety. Do not let the victim pull you into trouble.

3. If victim is beyond the reach of an extended article: Throw a line, a ring buoy, a spare tire, an inner tube or any buoyant object to the victim.

4. If victim is too far for reaching with an extended throw:
   Reach the victim in a boat. Row to him and extend oar or paddle. Pull the victim slowly to alongside the boat so that he can grasp the stern. Then pro-

pel the boat to safety. If the victim needs to be held, hold him in position until further help comes.

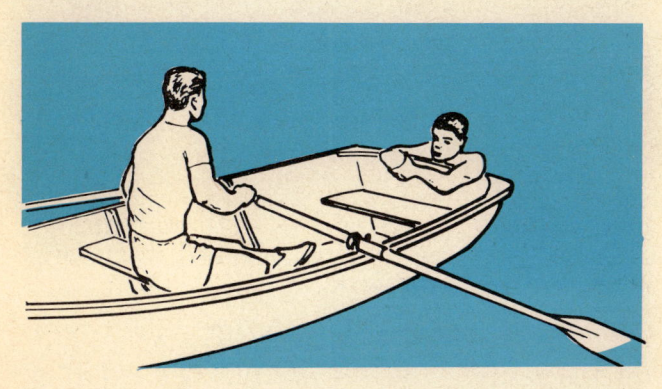

A swimmer untrained in lifesaving should swim to a victim in trouble only as a last resort and when all suggested safe resources have been exhausted. If it is necessary to risk swimming to a victim out of reach and no boat is available, the rescuer should take with him a loose towel, shirt, or any buoyant object to extend to the victim when he reaches him.

Helping Yourself in an Emergency

There are three basic rules for personal safety in emergencies: Do not panic. Think. Save your strength.

The following procedures are recommended for use in specific emergencies.

1. Cramps

The majority of cramps experienced in the water will be of the kind that affect the fingers, toes, arms, or legs and are usually caused by fatigue or overexertion. Cramps are of little danger to the swimmer unless they cause him to panic. If the victim will change his stroke and relax, this alone will many times bring relief. If the cramp continues, rubbing and kneading may help, but most important is the stretching of the muscle. If initiated as soon as a swimmer feels a distinct twitch or warning sign, the stretching process and change of stroke may cause relief.

Stomach cramps, which have been attributed to overexertion too soon after eating, are not common but they may occur. This kind of cramp, which might more accurately be called an abdominal cramp, need not be fatal or even as serious as was formerly believed. If the swimmer does not panic and will relax, stretch, and change his body position, he should still be successful in keeping afloat until the cramp is relieved.

2. Currents

When caught in a current, a victim should not attempt to buck or fight it. Instead, he should swim directly across the current. Even though this may bring him further downstream, it will enable him to reach safety without being exhausted.

3. Undertows, Runouts, and Rip Currents

Undertows, runouts, and rip currents tend to drag the swimmer away from the shore. The victim should not panic or struggle. Instead, he should swim parallel to shore across the current and, once free, swim to shore.

4. Weeds

When caught in weeds, the victim should not thrash or make a quick vigorous movement. Use of slow, careful movements will help to prevent further entanglement. A slow arm movement with just a gentle waving action of the legs is recommended.

5. Disrobing in the Water

A majority of drownings occur to people who find themselves accidentally in the water and fully clothed. In such cases the knowledge of how to disrobe in the water can be vitally important. The weight of water-soaked clothing impairs swimming efficiency, but in some instances it might be best not to disrobe. When safety is only a short distance away or there is the problem of cold water or when it is possible to safely hang onto a buoyant object, it might not be advisable to disrobe.

If the swimmer realizes that shirts and trousers can be easily inflated and act as flotation supports, it is readily seen that there is no need for panic. First of all, however, the shoes should be removed. To accomplish this, the swimmer takes a good breath and assumes a jellyfish float position. Then, using both hands, he removes one shoe at a time. When necessary, the head should be lifted long enough to take additional breaths as needed during this procedure.

6. Use of Clothing for Flotation

Close-woven materials that comprise most shirts and trousers hold trapped air when wet. The shirt can be inflated to give initial support. First, the shirt is buttoned at the collar and made tight at the neck. Then the swimmer takes a deep breath, bends the head forward, pulls the shirt up to the face, and exhales between the second and third button. The air will rise and form a bubble at the back of the shirt and give the needed support. The shirttail ends should be tied together at the waist, and in addition it may be necessary to grasp the shirt collar tight to prevent the escape of the trapped air.

Another method of inflating a shirt is by splashing air with the palm of the hand. To accomplish this skill, the swimmer floats on his back, holds the front of his shirttail with one hand, keeping it just under the surface. The free hand strikes downward from above the surface with the palm and continues the motion to a point below the shirttail. The air, carried downward from the surface, will bubble into the shirt, causing the inflation.

To use trousers or slacks for flotation, the swimmer takes a good breath, assumes a jellyfish float position, loosens the waistband or belt, and carefully and easily removes one leg of the clothing at a time. The head should be lifted high enough to take a breath as often as may be necessary. It is important not to hurry.

After the trousers are removed, the swimmer treads water and either ties both legs together at the cuff or ties a knot in each trouser leg as close to the bottom of the pants leg as possible. Then with the zipper pulled up, he grasps the back of the waistband with one hand and, with the trousers on the surface, splashes air into the open waist with the free hand. This is easily accomplished by striking down with the palm and following through to a point just below the open waist, which is kept below the surface.

Another simple method of inflating trousers is to submerge and blow air into the trousers through the waistband, which should be kept underwater. After the trousers have been inflated, the waistband can be gathered together by the hands or by tightening the belt if there is one.

The swimmer can now slip the head between the trouser legs near where they have been tied together, thus forming a Mae West type of flotation. If the legs are tied separately, the swimmer uses the inflated trousers as waterwings, which would be an equally serviceable improvised flotation support.

Survival Floating

The facedown floating technique described is adapted from the "drownproofing" technique that was originated by the late Fred R. Lanoue, former professor of physical education and head swimming coach at the Georgia Institute of Technology. This style of floating combines a series of basic swimming skills and is designed to keep a person afloat for a long period with a minimum of effort and energy.

The skill of survival floating can be performed as follows.

1. Resting Position

The swimmer starts with air in the lungs and holds his breath, letting his arms and legs dangle. The face is kept down so that the back of the head is at the surface. The swimmer rests and floats in this vertical position for a few seconds.

2. Preparing To Exhale

While maintaining this body and head position, the swimmer slowly and leisurely recovers or lifts the arms to about shoulder height. If leg action is also to be used, he slowly separates the legs into a modified scissors kick.

3. Exhalation

Making sure that the back of the head is still at the surface, the swimmer raises the head no higher than necessary for the mouth to clear the surface. At the same time, he exhales through the mouth and nose (some may exhale through mouth only or nose only). The eyes should be opened to help gauge and judge the head and body levels.

4. Inhalation

As soon as the head is vertical, the swimmer presses the arms downward and brings the legs together. This easy downward pressure should allow time for air to be breathed in through the mouth. The action of the arms and legs should not be vigorous enough to lift the chin out of the water.

5. Return to the Resting Position

The swimmer slowly allows the arms and legs to move back to their free dangling position, with face down in the water, and relaxes. He rests in this position until ready to exhale and then repeats the cycle. NOTE. If the individual tends to sink too far below the surface when going back to the dangling or resting position, a downward press or easy finning action of the arms will stop the sinking of the body and help float it back to the surface. A slight scissors kick can also be combined to arrest the sinking action.

10

FUN IN FUNDAMENTALS

It is an accepted fact that recreational aquatic activities play an important part in the swimming instruction program. This fact was ably demonstrated by Commodore W. E. Longfellow, the founder of the Red Cross Water Safety Program, who constantly applied a favorite motto "Keep the Fun in Fundamentals" and became an outstanding success as a teacher of swimming for people of all ages. The benefits of recreational aquatic activities are many. Such activities can be used effectively to overcome the fear of water that inhibits many children. They tend to relieve tension that can result from concentrated practice and effort. They may be used to create confidence and to teach skills. Many instructors use games as an excellent device for tapering off the formal instruction phase. Regardless of the choice of activity, the safety of the participants must always be a main consideration.

Selection of Activity

The instructor, or leader, must use judgment and discrimination in the selection of the activity. It should meet the needs of the group at that particular time. The game, contest, or stunt should be simple. Games and stunts for preschool children should revolve around simple play and fantasy. The very young can readily imagine themselves as characters in children's books and songs with which they are familiar. A prone glide can be a "torpedo"; a kicking race using kickboards can be playing "outboard motors"; finding and retrieving small weights from the bottom can be "finding hidden treasure"; exhaling can be "blowing bubbles." Most simple games can be adapted for shallow water for this age group.

Elementary school children have been exposed to class and group discipline and as a result they understand game rules and like to compete. Relays and simple team games that utilize skills they have learned or are learning should be emphasized.

Older children will enjoy games and contests that require a few more rules and strategy. Spelldown games requiring simple props and equipment can be used to advantage. Familiar land games are easily adapted since a larger playing area is practical and, depending on swimming ability, deeper water activity can be utilized. The least skilled swimmers may be placed in comparatively shallow depth of water or given a game responsibility that enables them to enjoy the activity in a manner commensurate with their ability.

In all recreational activities, the leader should plan the activity in advance. A simple and clear explanation of the activity plus an opportunity for the learner to ask questions will go a long way toward insuring the success of the fun period.

The following games and stunts are included to indicate the kind of activity that is suitable for the various swimming levels. Some are for individuals and some are for groups. Many land games can be adapted by the resourceful leader.

Individual Contests and Stunts at the Beginner and Advanced Beginner Levels

1. With face in water, touch toes as called for.
2. Sitting on bottom, exhale underwater (repeat 5 times).
3. Prone float to the counts of 10, 15, 20.
4. Prone glide for a distance of 10, 20, 30 feet.
5. Spread-eagle float on the back.
6. Glide for distance on the back. (Give points for each foot over 10 feet.)
7. Fin on the back for a distance of 15 feet.
8. Fin on the back in a 15-foot circle.

9. Race for 20 feet, face up, using a crawl kick glide.
10. Race for 25 feet, face down, using a crawl kick glide.
11. Race for 20 yards, face down, using a crawl stroke.
12. Race for 10 yards on the back, finning with a crawl kick.
13. Swim 10 yards on the front, do a roll-over, and swim 10 yards on the back.
14. Bob under 10 times in neck-deep water.
15. Swim 10 strokes and on cry of "shark" turn and swim back.
16. Shark game, varied by swimming to right and left.
17. Jump into deep water and swim back to shore using backstroke.
18. Jump into deep water; tread water for 15 seconds, using both arm and leg action.
19. Do a plain front header, swim 10 strokes, turn, swim to shore.
20. Float on the back (with or without finning) for 5 minutes.
21. Do a plain front dive and glide for distance.
22. Push off into a back glide and roll into a prone float.
23. Push off into a prone glide and roll into a face-up float.
24. Lying on back, fin feet forward for three body lengths.

Group Games and Contests at the Beginner Level

1. Catching ball in shallow water.
2. Passing water ball, standing in water.
3. Water dodge ball, in circle (promotes ducking).
4. Tunnel ball (passing ball back under the legs of several players).
5. Cat and mouse. (Cat is outside circle and mouse is inside.)
6. Poison tag.
7. Spoon and Ping-pong ball relay race.

8. Relay race in shallow water (running, gliding on front, gliding on back).
9. Kickboard race for 25 yards.
10. Kickboard relay for width of pool.
11. Circle catch. Players join hands in two or more circles of even numbers. A leader is chosen for each group. At a signal, each leader passes the ball to the left or the right. The object of the game is to see which side can pass the ball around the circle one or more times and get it back into the leader's hands first. If a contestant misses the ball he must recover it as quickly as possible.

Team Games for All Levels

Cork Game. The teams are lined up on opposite sides of the pool and 100 or more corks or floats are thrown into the water. At a signal, the teams swim toward the center and attempt to get as many of the corks as possible. The team collecting the greatest number in a given time wins.

Challenges. Challenges made between individuals within a group or leaders of different groups are always good fun. The challenger performs the stunt. If the opponent cannot do it, a point is scored for the challenger.

Drop the Puck. This game is played like drop the handkerchief except that a puck or other weighted object is used. The players form a circle around which "it" swims with the puck in his hand. He drops it behind one of the players, who must recover it and give chase around the circle, trying to catch "it" before he can succeed in taking his place.

Retrieving. Twenty or more bright tin plates or other objects are thrown into the water. Teams line up on shore. On a signal, teams dive in. The team recovering the greatest number of objects wins.

Volleyball. Any number of people may play. Players divide into two groups, one group on either side of a net that is hung so that the bottom is 2 or 3 feet above the water. Have players rotate from shallow to deep water if possible. A water polo ball is batted back and forth over the net by hitting it with the hands. Float lines can be used to mark the outside play area. Side loses the ball if it fails to return it or if it bats the ball over a limit line. Side winning the ball becomes the server. If the serving side wins the ball, it scores one point. Only the serving side scores; if it loses the ball it simply fails to score.

Punch Ball. A heavy wire is stretched down the middle of the pool and about 9 feet above the surface, running the length of the pool. Suspended from the cable on a sliding brass ring is a punch bag attached with a 7-foot rope and a snap buckle. The snap enables the leader to remove the bag when not in use. When attached, the bag hangs 1 foot above the surface. The playing group is divided into two teams, each of which remains on its side of the wire. The team batting the bag to its end of the pool scores a goal. In the melee the pool looks like a veritable "punch" bowl. Definite rules have not been worked out, but the game is good fun even without them.

Water Baseball. The "diamond" may be all deep water or all shallow water or only the outfield may be deep water. Use a plastic ball and bat.

Water Basketball. Goals are set 60 feet apart, or a shorter distance according to the size of the playing area. All play should be in deep water. The procedure is the same as in land basketball.

Tug of War. Prepare a long strip of heavy rope with stationary loops of heavy canvas to serve as shoulder loops, one for each swimmer. Tie a red cloth to mark the center of the rope. Float a rope for a center line. Players line up at rope, each adjusts one shoulder loop over his shoulder and, at a signal, they try to tug the rope toward their own goal. Each player has to swim hard against resistance. VARIATION. Two teams line up on shore. Two players hold a floated rope with center marked, parallel to the shore. At a signal, teams rush to rope and try to tug it to their side by swimming.

Mass Games

Swimming Spelldown. Leader calls out a stunt. Swimmers performing the stunt remain in the game; others are eliminated as in a spelling match until a champion is left. Start with easy stunts to prevent players being eliminated too fast and gradually make stunts more difficult.

Suggested stunts for a spelldown:
1. Swimming with one arm out (sidestroke).
2. Swimming on the back with both arms out.
3. Steamboat. (With body in extended glide position, feet perform crawl kick.)
4. Duck dive (surface dive).
5. Log roll. (Keep legs, body, and arms stretched in straight line; roll.)
6. Jackknife surface dive with hands kept at sides.
7. Corkscrew surface dive.
8. Marching on the water. (On back, move legs in walking motion, pressing lower leg back against the water on each "step.")
9. Sculling feetfirst, hands at side.
10. Sculling feetfirst, hands extended overhead.
11. Corkscrew sculling feetfirst.
12. Stomach-cramp float. (Rub stomach with both hands while floating on the back.)
13. Porpoise diving. (Surface dive to bottom, spring up for air, repeat.)
14. Crab swimming. (Move backwards by reversing arm action of the breaststroke.)
15. Crab swimming sideways. (On back, scull so as to move sideways.)
16. Mermaid's prayer. (Scull with body in a kneeling position.)
17. Waterwheel. (Scull on back so that the body rotates in a circle.)
18. Front somersault.
19. Back somersault.
20. Sculling on the back with one foot out of the water.
21. Sculling on the back with both feet out of the water.
22. The human bobber. (Balancing stunt. Take handstand position in deep water and scull so as to move forward, feet out of water.)

23. Swimming with hands clasped and feet together.
24. Pendulum float.
25. Bicycling on the side.
26. Treading water waist deep. (It requires strenuous treading to raise body in deep water so that the swimmer is treading with shoulders and chest out of water.)
27. Walking home from boat ride. (Perform waist-deep treading water and propel self forward.)
28. Rotary crawl. (Change alternately to front and back crawl on every arm stroke.)
29. Tasmanian crawl. (Swimmer is on his side with one arm extended in front of the head and the other alongside the body. The hands flop on the surface, and the swimmer moves forward using a flutter kick.)

Neptune's Call. Players are lined up on one side of the pool. The one who is "it" stands or treads water in the center of the pool. When he shouts, "Neptune's call, come one and all," the players must swim to the opposite side, and he tries to tag as many as he can. All the players tagged must remain in the center and help in tagging the others until all are caught.

Pigeon. Everyone sits at the edge of the water or side of the pool with the knees under the chin and hands clasped around the legs. At the leader's signal, players dive in and swim to the other side of the pool; those who reach there last become "pigeons" and must drop out of the game. (Leader designates the number of players who will be classified as "last.") At camp, the game may be played from the side of a raft, and the players can swim around it. This is a fine game to give learners practice in getting into and out of the water and to test their swimming and diving ability.

Leapfrog. Players line up, starting in shallow water, with those in deep water treading. The end player on each line puts his hands on the shoulders of the player in front of him, pushing him underwater while he leaps over with legs widespread. Procedure is continued until the former first-in-line becomes last. This is a fine game to make swimmers feel at home in the water and can be played as a team game too.

Pom-Pom Pullaway. Players line up on one side of pool or swimming area. "It" is on the opposite side (called the line). When "it" calls out "Pom-Pom Pullaway," players must swim across to opposite side, while "it" tries to catch them before they reach the line. Those who are tagged must join "it" and try to tag the others.

Poison. Players form a ring by joining hands or by grasping an endless rope. "Poison" is some floating object anchored in the center of the group. The aim of the action is to pull others so that they touch poison but keep from touching it themselves. Anyone touching poison is eliminated from the ring until only one person is left. NOTE. This and other circle games can be played in shallow water by children. They have value in getting beginners adjusted to the water.

Water Tactics (Grand March, Etc.). Group, in deep water, executes movements at command of leader, who orders facings, marchings, and salutes for individuals. In rows of two or four, groups execute marching, wheelings, etc., in parade style.

Stunt Tag. Leader calls out a certain part of the body, and a player is safe from being tagged when that part of the body is out of water. "It" may tag any player not thus immunized, and the person tagged becomes "it." VARIATION. The leader calls out more than one body part, as, for example, "head submerged and hand out," "both feet out."

Ball Tag. This game is played in a limited area, in water waist deep for nonswimmers or in deep water for swimmers. "It" tries to tag someone by tossing the ball. The one who is tagged becomes "it."

Japanese Tag. Leader announces a certain part of body that must be tagged by "it." Those who are tagged must join "it" and try to tag the remaining players.

Hold Tag. The one who is "it" walks or swims after the players, attempting to tag them. The player tagged must place his left hand on the spot where he was touched and, holding this position, attempt to tag someone else.

Will-o'-the-Wisp. This very interesting game is preferably played with six or eight swimmers. All are blindfolded except one person who is "it" and has a bell. "It" submerges and swims underwater. Each time he surfaces he must ring the bell, and those blindfolded try to tag him. The player who tags the bellman becomes "it" and gets the bell. The tagged player joins the blindfolded group, and the game continues. A whistle may be substituted for the bell.

Under Cover (Duck Under). This is a variation tag game. In order to be safe from being tagged, the players must be completely submerged.

Relay Races

Variations. Any of the events described as racing events under "Individual Contests and Stunts at the Beginner Level" may be used as relay races when desired.

Leapfrog Relay. Teams line up in shallow water, and a goal is designated in deep water. At a signal, the player in the last position on each team leaps over the players in front of him one at a time and then swims to the goal. When he has reached the goal, the player who is now in the last position starts the same leapfrog process, and the relay continues until all team members have reached the goal.

Obstacle Relay. Teams line up on the shore. At a signal the first swimmer in each team races to a log anchored in the water, climbs over the log, turns and swims under it, and returns to the start. Then the second swimmer follows suit, and the procedure is repeated in turn by the remaining team members. Other obstacles might be barrels, spars, life buoys, or other flotation devices.

Disrobing Relay. The first swimmer in each team wears an assortment of clothing over his bathing suit. Such clothing may be pajamas or a complete street outfit. At a signal, he dives in, swims to a raft or other side of pool, climbs out, disrobes, and returns to the starting point. On his return, the second swimmer goes to the raft or poolside, climbs out, and dresses in the outfit discarded by the first swimmer.

Touch Relay. Teams line up on opposite sides. The object of the game is to touch whatever the leader calls out and return to the starting place as quickly as possible. The leader may involve any number of skills learned or a combination of skills by calling out "touch bottom," "touch toes," "touch float line," etc.

Swim-the-Duck Relay. A wooden decoy duck for each team is the only equipment used. The "duck" is carried in a swimming position on the surface by one hand, requiring each team member to swim with other hand and legs. "Ducks" must not be submerged or clutched against swimmer's body and must be advanced toward the goal at all times.

Flag Relay. This event is designed to develop and utilize the side-carry position employed in lifesaving. A small flag may be carried in the upper hand and passed to teammates in the water. VARIATION. Swimmers, in turn, carry a large parade flag (a 6-foot flag on an 8-foot staff); the base of the staff rests on the swimmer's upper hip. The flag is carried upright and must be kept dry. Red Cross flags, flags with aquatic symbols, or international flags may be used. Shallow arm pull and scissors kick must be used.

11

ARTIFICIAL RESPIRATION

The majority of drowning accidents occur in unsupervised water areas. The tremendous increase in the number of farm ponds, impounded bodies of water, reservoirs, and residential pools, where no trained lifeguard or qualified first aider is on duty, makes it the concern of everyone to be able to care for himself and others in the event of an accident or sudden emergency. Training in emergency first aid procedures and lifesaving skills is offered free of charge by most American Red Cross chapters.

When a victim is rescued after immersion and is unconscious and apparently not breathing, immediate help is needed. Because of its simplicity and effectiveness, the mouth-to-mouth method of artificial resuscitation is recommended for all cases requiring artificial respiration.

Artificial Respiration for Water Cases

Individuals who die as a result of a water accident usually die from the lack of air, not because of the presence of water in the lungs or the stomach.

A victim who is drowning may be either active or passive. Unless unconscious, the drowning victim struggles to remain on the surface or to regain the surface in order to secure air. Such effort is energy-consuming and may result in the victim swallowing varying quantities of water. This water, along with food remaining in the stomach, could, if regurgitated, obstruct the air passages and interfere with the efforts of the rescuer. The possibility of an obstruction must be recognized by the rescuer and immediate steps taken if an obstruction should occur. Also, evaporation of water from the victim's skin will result in lowering still further a body temperature that may already be dangerously low. It is imperative, therefore, to keep the victim from becoming chilled. Artificial respiration should be started immediately after rescue, even in the water if possible, and does not depend upon special equipment for its application.

The following procedure should be followed to adequately ventilate the lungs of a nonbreathing victim.

1. Quickly clear the mouth of any foreign matter that might be visible.

2. Tilt the head back so that the chin is pointing upward. This maneuver should provide for an open airway by moving the tongue away from the back of the throat. (If additional clearance is needed later, it may be necessary to pull or push the jaw upward into a jutting-out position.)
3. Open your mouth wide and place it tightly over the mouth of the victim. Pinch the victim's nostrils shut

and blow into his mouth. If the airway is clear, only a moderate resistance to the blowing effort is felt, and the victim's chest will visibly expand.

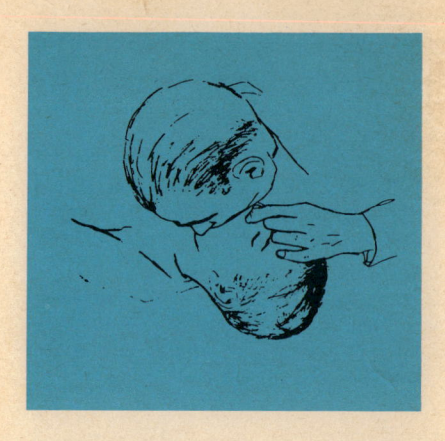

4. Remove your mouth and allow the air to escape. Repeat the blowing effort. For an adult, blow vigorously at the rate of about 12 breaths a minute. For a child, take relatively shallow breaths 20 times a minute. For an infant, place your mouth over the victim's mouth and nose and give shallow puffs of air about 20 times a minute. If resistance to the blowing effort is experienced, recheck the head position and hold the jaw forward.

Should the airway remain blocked, quickly turn the victim on his side and administer several sharp blows between the shoulder blades in the hope of dislodging the foreign matter. Clear the mouth while the victim is still on his side. Infants and small children should be suspended head downward when an attempt is made to clear the airway.

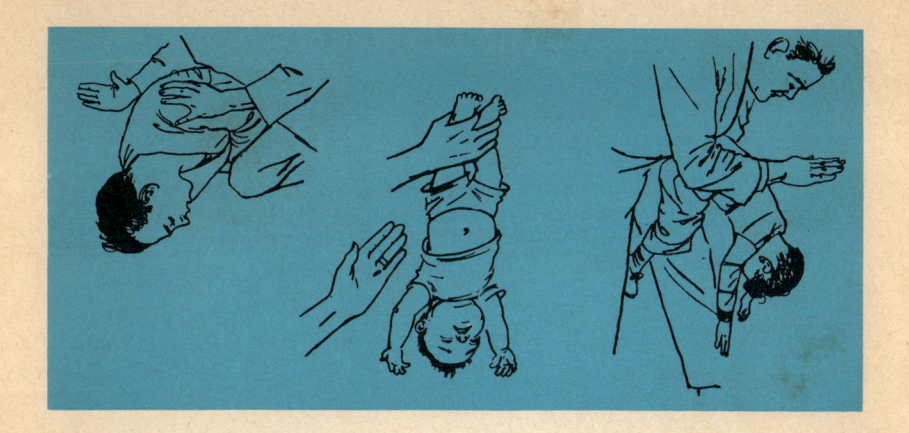

Related Information

The efforts of the rescuer should be timed to coincide with the victim's first attempt to breathe for himself.

If vomiting occurs, the victim should be quickly turned on his side, the mouth wiped out, and then repositioned to continue the blowing effort.

Normally, recovery should be rapid, except in electric shock, drug poisoning, or carbon monoxide poisoning cases. In these instances, nerves and muscles controlling the breathing system are paralyzed or deeply depressed or the carbon monoxide has displaced oxygen in the bloodstream over a period of time. When these cases are encountered, artificial respiration must often be carried on for long periods.

When a victim is revived, he should be kept as quiet as possible until he is breathing regularly. He should be kept covered and otherwise treated for shock until suitable transportation is available, if he must be moved.

Artificial respiration should be continued until the victim begins to breathe for himself or until a physician pronounces the victim dead or until the person appears to be dead beyond any doubt.

A doctor's care is necessary during the recovery period, as respiratory and other disturbances may develop as an aftermath.

Excessive inflation pressure or improper opening of the air passage can cause air to distend the stomach. Slight distension may be disregarded. If there is marked distension, effort should be made to relieve the condition. Using one hand, exert moderate pressure just below the rib cage. Turn the victim's head to the side to avoid possible aspiration of stomach contents. Slight pressure may be applied over the stomach area by an assistant to prevent repeated stomach inflation.

Other American Red Cross safety textbooks and publications available for purchase from chapters are —
Life Saving and Water Safety, Stock No. 321102
Teaching Johnny To Swim, Stock No. 321126
Canoeing, Stock No. 321125
Basic Canoeing, Stock No. 321140
Basic Rowing, Stock No. 321141
Basic Sailing, Stock No. 321143
First Aid Textbook, Paperbound, Stock No. 321101
First Aid Textbook, Clothbound, Stock No. 321100
Basic First Aid Books 1, 2, 3, 4, Stock No. 321148